Astrology for a Yogi

How to use the stars for intuitive guidance and happiness

Kashiraja
(Massimo Barbagallo)

Copyright © 2012 Massimo Barbagallo

All rights reserved.

ISBN-10: 1481840649
ISBN-13: 978-1481840644

Cover: Paramhansa Yogananda. The photo in the background is of a collision between two clusters of galaxies and was taken by NASA with a space telescope; it is considered a proof of the existence of dark matter, called dark because nobody, in 2012, is sure of what it really is.

Contents

1. The stars and free will   7
2. Signs, elements and modalities   11
3. Signs and planets   16
4. Planets and chakras   20
5. Opposite signs   25
6. Planets and yoga   36
7. Planets and houses   38
8. Signs and houses   45
9. Groups of houses   49
10. Houses and elements   57
11. Planets and deities   61
12. Rahu and Ketu   68
13. Kashiraja's chart   77
14. Planets and the Bhagavad Gita   88
15. Adelle's chart   92
16. Planetary friendships   100
17. The stars in each moment   105
18. Signs and the Gita   109
19. Kate's chart   115
20. Shifu's chart   122
21. Navamsha   127
22. Relative planetary placements   134
23. Chart of Paramhansa Yogananda   139
24. Chart of Swami Kriyananda   144
25. Vimshottari dasha   149
26. Transits   160
27. Positional strength   167
28. Planetary yogas   169
29. Gems and mantras   174
30. Nakshatras   180
31. Nakshatras and vimshottari dasha   202
32. Chart calculations   203
33. Interpreting a chart   206
References   209

Charts

Signs, elements and modalities   14
Planets and chakras   24
Mahatma Gandhi   27
Lahiri Mahasaya   28
Anne   39
Houses   49
Kashiraja   79
Adelle   94
A chart for a moment   107
Kate   116
Shifu   123
Kashiraja's navamsha   130
Paramhansa Yogananda   141
Swami Kriyananda   145
First group of nakshatras   181
Second group of nakshatras   188
Third group of nakshatras   194

It is never a question of belief; the only scientific attitude one can take on any subject is whether it is true. Swami Sri Yukteswar

Paramhansa Yogananda (right) with his guru Swami Sri Yukteswar.

This book is based on the teachings of Paramhansa Yogananda, spiritual master and author of *Autobiography of a yogi;* of his guru, Sri Yukteswar, astrologer; of his guru's guru Lahiri Mahasaya; of Yogananda's direct disciple, Swami Kriyananda; on the astrology classes of Drupada (John Macdonald); and on the helpful editing of my wife, Viktoriya.

Names which appear with a * on their first mention have been changed for privacy.
312 Dwapara (A.D. 2012)

PS: in this book I sometimes use the british rather than the american spelling, for instance practise instead of practice.

Chapter One

The stars and free will

It is not our passing thoughts or brilliant ideas but our everyday habits that control our lives. Paramhansa Yogananda

At any one time, we are influenced by many things in our life, some by our own choice, others definitely not of our choosing! Do we really need to add the stars to the list? Not really, and many people go on rather well with their lives without thinking of the stars except for the occasional glance at a beautiful night sky. Astrology, though, is a way to understand our consciousness and that of others. Anybody who has gone through a moment of "grrr, you do not tell me what to do! I decide!" has experienced the energy of Aries, who likes to be independent but can be harsh – depending on whether we express its positive or negative side. Similarly, other states of consciousness are described by other signs and planets.

Astrology is a language, a description of energies we experience every day. My intention is to describe this language with sufficient clarity for everybody to connect it with that experience we all possess; with this connection we can use astrology to express with the clarity of intuition the energy we are experiencing. That is how, when given the chart of a person, a good astrologer can intuit and describe some characteristics of that person.

We all feel and experience the energy of other people, it is not a special skill of the astrologer. One difference though is that astrology gives one way (not the only way) to describe this experience. Another difference is that good astrologers specifically train themselves to listen to intuition when reading a chart. However, this book is on astrology for a *yogi*. Yogis, in their practice of yoga

Chapter One

and meditation, also learn to develop their intuition. All good astrologers are yogis; all good yogis can be astrologers.

Yoga teaches that the only obstacle to true and lasting happiness is actually in our mind, in those habitual thoughts that keep us separated from our spiritual joyful essence. Yogananda said: "Habits are mental mechanisms which enable us to act automatically, leaving our consciousness free for other duties. A habit is formed by several attentive repetitions of an action." Habits of success, failure, sorrow, or happiness are all stored in our mind, originating from past and present actions; they influence our free will and in turn they can be reinforced or dissolved by fresh acts of willpower.

Every act of will, every thought, every habit is made of energy and is subtly linked to the stars; astrology then consists in understanding our habits and the way we are using our free will.

In the widest sense, astrology is part of the vast knowledge of yoga. Neither yoga nor astrology fully explains why or how a subtle link exists between us and the stars, but exist it does. Yoga however does describe some details about this link and its influence on our aura.

The aura is our energetic body, where all thoughts and habits exist as patterns of energy; it has energy channels and centers which focus on specific aspects of consciousness. For example, the heart energy center, in the middle of the chest, is where a great part of our feelings is centered; even our very language describes this fact, in expressions such as heartbroken and heartwarming. In astrology we learn this center is connected to Venus, so the position of Venus in our birth chart tells us something about how we relate to feelings such as loyalty, idealism, affection and love. Venus in Pisces, a sensitive and expansive sign, might indicate a generously lovable attitude, while in Virgo, a sign inclined to wisdom and rationality, it might indicate a more discriminative and cautious approach.

Different groups of stars and planets resonate with different parts of our aura, forming a link between us and the stars. Through this link we feel and *respond* to the energy of the stars. This is the first and most important thing to keep in mind, in the words of Sri Yukteswar: "Astrology is the study of our response to the

The stars and free will

planetary stimuli."

Our response is a mixture of free will and habit. Habits are energetic patterns which we have formed in the past by repeated actions; they can be good or bad, and we can change them by willpower. Bad habits do not bring us any true happiness, only a false and temporary version of it. To change them, however, we need to be aware of them. Together with introspection, an astrological chart can help a yogi because it shows the strongest good and bad habits that we possess. By acquiring new awareness, we can better use our free will to choose the best response to our life situations; it is the way we respond that greatly influences their outcome. Even if a challenge is particularly difficult, we can always at least improve our state of mind. This inner response has the greatest importance in actually changing the external circumstances, as it will magnetically attract a positive outcome. Paramhansa Yogananda said: "...you must realize that thoughts are things. The very universe, in the final analysis, is composed not of matter but of consciousness. Matter responds, far more than most people realize, to the power of thought. For will power directs energy, and energy in return acts upon matter. Matter, indeed, is energy."

At the time of our birth, the planets will be in a certain configuration in the sky. This configuration will play a special role in our life as it shows some of the most important lessons we have come to learn. If we have a strong planet in an harmonious position, it will be a supportive energy; if a planet is weak or in a challenging position, it will indicate an area where we are acting, to some degree, with ego-consciousness. The ego is the soul identified with the body, so to find spiritual freedom we need to learn to expand our consciousness beyond the ego, overcoming any challenging astrological influence.

For example, Mercury is the planet of intellect and Pisces is its most challenging sign because the two energies are not immediately harmonious: Pisces is a water sign and water signifies feelings and emotions; Pisces is also the most open and sensitive of the three water signs. The ego is very much concerned with emotions, so if we are trying to use our intellect for some rational thinking process,

Chapter One

such as studying science, and we have a habit of concentrating too much on our emotions (anxiety, frustration...), we will not be very successful. If, however, we make an effort to calm our mind, we will respond to the energy of Mercury in Pisces more on the inner soul level. When our feelings are truly calm, they'll manifest as intuition. Mercury in Pisces then shows a perceptive and intuitional thinker.

Any strengthening influence in the chart will facilitate our efforts. For example, Pisces is a sign of Jupiter, so Jupiter positioned there with Mercury will support it, as planets in their own sign share their strength. Intuition is an important quality in scientific research, and I know two people with Mercury and Jupiter in Pisces who have done successful research at university level.

How good is our response to this planetary energy, or any other, depends on our effort, every moment, and our increasing attunement to Spirit. A meditation technique will raise our consciousness, calm our mind and increase our attunement.

Ultimately a technical knowledge of the meanings of the planets and signs is not sufficient to interpret an astrological chart: the true key is developing one's intuition, which is primarily done by meditation and other spiritual practices, and by striving at all times to listen to inner guidance.

Chapter Two

Signs, elements and modalities

As we learn the language of astrology we will gain familiarity with different words and concepts, but the essential alphabet will remain the twelve signs.

The signs of the zodiac are groups of stars with specific characteristics; each of the planets is always under the influence of the sign it occupies, that is why they form the basis of astrology.

A person's chart is made of all twelve signs, some of which will be more prominent than others, but before we are able to handle the complexity of a chart we need to learn at least some of the individual qualities of each sign.

The most fundamental trait of a sign is its element: fire, earth, air or water. The elements are a useful concept as they are a good way to remember, or derive anew, the qualities of each sign. A basic meaning for fire is energy, earth is material form, air is intellect, and water is feelings. If we know a sign is fiery, we know that it will be energetic; if too energetic, it may have a quick temper, while if the sign has some difficulty, it may indicate lack of energy.

Similarly, if a sign is earthy it will be stable, but it may be too stable (stubborn) or not stable enough (lacking confidence). Air signs will be smart and mentally agile, but may be aloof and scattered. Water signs are receptive and intuitive, but they may also be oversensitive and emotional.

By just applying this simple concept we can already do some chart interpretation: if a chart has a strong fire sign, we know that the person will be energetic and willful. If in the same chart there are no planets in water signs, we also know that this person, unless they are spiritually advanced, needs to balance their fiery willpower with receptivity and sensitivity for others. Willpower is a gift, but it can be misused if we lack balance. The sensitivity of water signs can balance the fiery determination of fire signs, so if a chart has strong fire signs but no strength in water signs it would likely indicate an imbalance. Being aware of this fact, we could pay extra attention and cultivate our kindness and receptivity.

The elements are not just theoretical ideas, they are states of consciousness which are part of our everyday life, whether we are aware of them or not. They are even part of our mainstream culture: in the commercially successful *Avatar: The Last Airbender*, a funny and well written TV cartoon, the world is comprised of four nations, each for a different element. A perceptive character describes the elements like this: "Fire is the element of power. The people of the fire nation have desire and will, and the energy and drive to achieve what they want. Earth is the element of substance. The people of the earth kingdom are diverse and strong. They are persistent and enduring. Air is the element of freedom. The air nomads detach themselves from worldly concerns and find peace and freedom. Also, apparently they have pretty good senses of humour! Water is the element of change. The people of the water tribe are capable of adapting to many things. They have a deep sense of community and love that holds them together through anything."

The zodiac is generally considered to start with Aries, because it is the sign most akin to beginnings. Aries, if expressed in a positive and spiritually mature way, is energetic, dynamic, willful and independent. You could have guessed, it is a fire sign. I have a strong Aries in my chart, so I can be quite fiery; in fact, it is something that people note in me even when they have no knowledge of astrology.

After Aries we have an earth sign, Taurus. Taurus is stable, determined and nourishing, clearly earthy qualities, if we visualize the strength of rocks as well as the softness of wet and nurturing soil. Next is Gemini, an air sign; it is perceptive and subtle in understanding and communicating. Air is free to go anywhere, and freedom is necessary for any effective intellectual exploration. Then we find Cancer, whose element is water. Cancer is intuitive, affectionate and caring. Calm water has a gentle and soothing touch.

The sequence of elements of the first four signs, fire, earth, air,

Signs, elements and modalities

water, is repeated twice more to complete the circle of twelve. Leo is then a fire sign, inspiring, bright and powerful. Virgo is earthy, incisive, discriminating, pure and calm. Libra is airy, idealistic, diplomatic and harmonious. Scorpio, a water sign, is deep, dedicated and mystical.

Sagittarius is fiery, enthusiastic, joyful and expansive. Capricorn is earthy, resolute, focused and practical. Aquarius is airy, impersonal, detached, wise and humanitarian. Pisces is watery, empathic, compassionate, insightful and universal.

We can often use our instinctive experience of the elements to perceive some characteristics of a sign, however there are twelve signs and four elements. How do we distinguish among the three signs of the same element? One difference is the planet they are associated with. Each sign is in special harmony with one planet, which in astrology is said to own it, or rule it. Cancer, the water sign ruled by Moon, is likely to be more sociable and gentle than Scorpio, the water sign ruled by Mars. This is because Moon is a gentle and sensitive planet, while Mars is fiery and willful.

To understand a sign we need to blend the characteristics of its element with those of the planet that rules it. Both Cancer and Scorpio are water signs, so they both have an innate capacity to be sensitive, however they'll manifest that quality in different ways because of their planetary ruler.

Cancer can have intense feelings, but it's gentle, while Scorpio is passionate.

Another difference among signs is their modality. The three signs of the same element will each have a distinct way of expression: active, fixed, or mutable. This is their modality. For example, Aries, Leo and Sagittarius are the three fire signs: Aries is active, Leo is fixed and Sagittarius is mutable. A basic description of each modality is suggested by its very name: active signs are naturally dynamic in expression, fixed signs are more stable, and mutable signs are more subtle and sensitive. This is their nature, how we respond to it, though, is our choice. Feeling the influence of an active sign, we might swiftly act at the right time, or feel under pressure and impulsively rush our actions. When a sign is fixed, it can mean depth, or excessive focus. Mutable signs can give subtleness, or be swayed too easily.

Just like the sequence of four elements is repeated three times around the zodiac, the sequence of three modalities is repeated four times, again starting from Aries, which is active. Taurus is fixed, and Gemini mutable; then Cancer will be active and so on. As a consequence, each of the twelve signs has a unique combination of element and modality: Aries is active fire; Taurus, fixed earth; Gemini, mutable air; Cancer, active water, and so on.

Pisces *mutable water*	Aries *active fire*	Taurus *fixed earth*	Gemini *mutable air*
Aquarius *fixed air*			Cancer *active water*
Capricorn *active earth*			Leo *fixed fire*
Sagittarius *mutable fire*	Scorpio *fixed water*	Libra *active air*	Virgo *mutable earth*

Signs, elements and modalities.
In the South Indian notation the position of the signs is always the same, so it is not written explicitly in a chart. Throughout this book, Aries will be the 2nd square from the top left, continuing clockwise with the rest of the signs.

Many qualities of a sign can be understood simply through its element and mode of expression, instead of memorizing its many characteristics. By learning the twelve elemental modalities we can use them to find inspiration in understanding a chart. For example, Aries is active fire. Fire is energy, and dynamic energy is needed for new beginnings. The element and mode of expression

Signs, elements and modalities

of Aries suggest it has an innate capacity to start anew after any failure.

We should not draw conclusions from a superficial application of this classification: a wise person with many planets in fixed signs will be more dynamic and subtle than a spiritually immature person with many planets in active and mutable signs. Our consciousness has divine resources which are not bound by the energy of the stars.

We will learn about the signs organically throughout this book, rather than having here at the beginning a list of twelve chapters summarizing the qualities of each sign. One reason I do this is that it lets us start with chart interpretation earlier, without having to first go through a great number of introductory chapters. Another reason is that Swami Kriyananda describes the twelve signs in his book *The Sun Sign as a Spiritual Guide*. Rather than duplicate his excellent description, I will go over the same concepts in a different manner, and integrate them with other elements of astrology he did not describe in detail. In any case, if you want to deepen your understanding of the signs you should really pick up his book!

Chapter Three

Signs and planets

The Earth is surrounded by stars in all directions, however in astrology we only look at a narrow band of stars which encircles our planet like a ring. All the planets in the solar system always appear to move within this narrow band, the zodiac, which is divided into twelve constellations or signs. The planets are much closer to Earth than the stars of the zodiac; they are considered to be within a sign only energetically, not physically.

Why twelve signs? The reason is understood by observing the movement of the Sun and Moon in our sky.

As seen from Earth, the Sun travels across the sky from dawn to sunset, against the distant backdrop of the zodiac. The zodiac also appears to rotate from east to west, but at a pace slightly slower than the Sun. Because the zodiac and the Sun circle the Earth at almost the same speed, the Sun takes a long time to move from constellation to constellation. The amount of time it takes for the Sun to make one lap around the zodiac is one year.

At the same time, the Moon goes through its recurring phase cycle in our sky, waxing from new to full and waning from full to new. Normally there are twelve Moon cycles in one year (only occasionally there will be thirteen), so a division into twelve parts is naturally suggested by the two astronomical bodies most visible from Earth: the Sun and the Moon. A year is divided into twelve months, and the zodiac is divided into twelve signs or constellations.

There are nine astrological planets which are directly relevant to us; five of them rule two signs each, while Sun and Moon rule one sign each; the last two of them do not rule any sign. Though the planets move around the zodiac all the time, they always maintain a special connection to their own signs, so it is useful to keep their association in mind.

Signs and planets

Aries and Scorpio are signs of Mars. Mars is fiery, willful, determined, independent and combative; it is not innately sensitive or receptive.

Taurus and Libra are ruled by Venus. Venus is sensitive, charming, benefic and perceptive; it can be overly sensual if spiritually immature, and a little attached to material things.

Gemini and Virgo are ruled by Mercury. Mercury is witty, mentally agile and insightful; it can become overly restless and scattered if overloaded with rational thoughts and worries.

Cancer is the sign of the Moon. Moon shows how we feel, it is a sensitive planet; it can become too emotional and oversensitive, and a little attached.

Leo is ruled by the Sun. Sun is fiery, willful and inspiring; it can become too authoritative and overly proud.

Sagittarius and Pisces are ruled by Jupiter. Jupiter is generous, intuitive, enthusiastic and compassionate; it can lack direction and common sense if undeveloped.

Capricorn and Aquarius are signs of Saturn. Saturn is focused, steadfast, impersonal and detached; it can be too cold and critical if its energy is not spiritually oriented.

The last two of the nine planets, Rahu and Ketu, have no physical counterpart though they are related to the orbit of the Moon around the Earth; they are always exactly opposite each other in a chart. Rahu directs our energy into the world: a mature expression would be compassionate service to others, otherwise Rahu makes us scattered and restless. Ketu is introspective; if positive it will be insightful, otherwise it will be oversensitive.

The signs rise in the east and move across the sky to the west, following the progression of the zodiac at a speed similar to the Sun, so they complete a full rotation around the Earth in about a day. It takes roughly between one and three hours for a sign to completely rise on the horizon, though the exact pace changes throughout the day and the year. The point in the east where the signs and planets rise is of special importance in astrology and is called the ascendant.

When we draw a chart we want to study the movement of the planets relative to the signs, so we consider the signs as fixed and

Chapter Three

use them as a reference frame. From this reference, the ascendant moves in the chart just like another planet.

The planets and the ascendant have differing speeds, though. The ascendant moves faster than any planet, spending roughly between one and three hours in each sign. The Sun takes one month to cross one sign, similarly to Mercury and Venus, while Mars spends about two months in each sign. Then there are the slower planets: Jupiter spends one year in each sign; Rahu and Ketu a year and a half; Saturn a little over two years.

Moon is the fastest planet as it moves across the twelve signs in one month, spending two days and a fraction in each. The Moon changes phase constantly, so its influence is changeable. The full Moon is more outgoing and strong, its lit side fully visible to us; the new Moon turns inward and is more introspective, it is dark. A full Moon, or a Moon that is waxing, can encourage expression in the material world. A new Moon, or a waning Moon, shines its light on the inner world. A waning or waxing Moon can be equally good for a yogi; what is important is how we respond to its energy. Moon is our mind and feelings: a positive response to its position in a chart gives a calm and happy mind, a negative response gives restlessness and unhappiness.

The phases of the Moon represent the ever changing cycle of nature. Because the Moon is changeable, it can also be adaptable. Experiencing change continuously, it can adapt to circumstances better than other planets like the usually slow and methodical Saturn, or willful Sun.

Each of the nine planets will blend its energy with the sign it occupies, and will exert an influence on our aura. For example, during its apparent circular motion in the sky, the Sun crosses the sign of Leo once per year. Leo is the sign of the Sun: they have many qualities in common and are in natural harmony. Everyone, to some degree, will feel this influence, however, if you happen to be born during this time, you'll respond to it in a very special manner. Of the three fire signs, Leo displays the deepest and most fixed characteristics. Fire shines light around it and can be charming and warming. If we feel as if this energy belongs to us, and it is *exclusively* the product of our own accomplishments, we

Signs and planets

might feel proud and entitled to recognition. By focusing on the outward effects of our shining energy, we will probably not be very sensitive to how others respond to it – only whether they show some kind of appreciation. Leo likes to be appreciated! We might also not be too keen on listening, we want to be listened to. To the degree, however, that we pay attention to the subtle origin of this fiery energy, which comes from Spirit inside, we will be a pure channel of its expression. By responding to Leo at a soul level, and not at an ego level, we are able to develop its positive qualities: self-confidence, strength and insightful perception. Leo radiates like the Sun and it can be very inspirational, helping others to develop those same positive qualities.

The Sun is an important planet for everyone, as it signifies our soul, vitality and capacity for self-expression. The Sun shines, and so it represents the way we shine in our life, and how we express ourselves to others.

The Sun and the Moon are the most personal planets – the Moon even more so than the Sun. When interpreting a chart, the Moon is of primary importance as it shows our feelings and state of mind.

However the ascendant, the east at our birth, takes precedence over the Sun and Moon in chart interpretation. East is where the Sun is born every day and at any time of day or night the east represents the birth of that moment. The rising Sun is blessing us with its light, and east is the direction from where spiritual blessings shine at all times; that is why yogis are advised to meditate facing east, if possible. The ascendant then, the east at our birth, is very influential in a chart; it is subtly settled between dualities: sky and earth, spirit and matter, and represents the door for the manifestation of our soul on earth.

The ascendant takes on the characteristics of the sign it occupies, and will influence the whole chart: if it is strong, the chart will be strong; if it lacks strength, we will need to exert more energy to realize our efforts. If your ascendant is not strong, though, do not worry: there are many yoga techniques that can strengthen your mind and aura, which is the same as strengthening your ascendant.

Chapter Four

Planets and chakras

The signs and planets have a subtle influence on our aura, as they are connected to energy centers along the energetic spine. The main energy channel of our aura, the energetic spine, runs straight through our body, roughly where the physical spine is, though it is straight and does not have the slight S shape followed by the vertebrae. Along the energetic spine there are energy centers called chakras, an important concept in yoga: yoga techniques aim to liberate the flow of energy in the spine going through the chakras. The stronger the upward flow, the stronger our aura.

Yogananda explained that each chakra corresponds to a planet and its signs: Mars, for example, corresponds to the 3rd chakra. By studying Mars and its two signs in our chart, we can learn about our 3rd chakra. In other words, by studying our chart we are studying our aura. Conversely, by studying the chakras we can learn some general characteristics of the planets and signs.

The position of the planets in our chart shows our energetic habits. While we cannot change the position of the planets and the nature of the signs, we can certainly change our aura. We can change our response to the stars, and we can learn to transcend their influence altogether.

To continue our example, Aries is ruled by Mars and it is the active fire sign: it has energy, drive and motivation. The active modality is creative. Fire radiates outward, so it directs energy into motion. Being active fire, Aries is apt at starting new things with enthusiasm. Sri Yukteswar had a strong Aries and he expressed perfectly the independent character of this sign; he had Mars, Sun, Mercury and Rahu all in Aries. Although of gentle nature, he was also known for the oft cauterizing words directed at those who sought his counsel. For those with a strong Aries who do not yet

Planets and chakras

possess the wisdom of a spiritual master, it is especially important to learn self-control, and to behave, or we may utter insensitive words and be impatient and bossy. Masters have achieved perfect self-control and their words, even if at times seemingly harsh, never originate from harsh feelings, only from genuine concern for others' well-being.

Now, in yoga it is explained that the 3rd chakra expresses the fire element in our aura. Fire is energy and self-control is important to direct it.

A similar consideration is obviously valid for Aries, which is a fire sign, however Scorpio is a water sign, so what is its connection to the 3rd chakra?

Scorpio is ruled by Mars and even though it is a water sign, it can also be fiery and intense, but not in an obvious way like Aries. The waters of Scorpio run deep and silent, but with power: Scorpio also needs to develop self-control, like Aries.

Similarly to Mars and the 3rd chakra, a subtle connection exists between the other planets, their signs and the other chakras. To understand it, we need to distinguish between the elements of the chakras and that of the signs. Just like each zodiacal sign has its own element, each chakra has an element which defines its qualities. This element, though, is distinct from that of the two signs which are connected to that chakra. For example, the element of Aries is fire and that of Scorpio is water, while the element of the 3rd chakra is fire.

The elements of the first four chakras are earth, water, fire, and air, but the higher chakras have a more subtle nature so their elements do not have physical counterparts; they are ether, super-ether, and pure light.

The elements of the chakras go from pure light at top of the spine, to earth at the base of the spine, symbolizing the material manifestation of Spirit through progressively denser elements. However, this is not to say that the earth element is not spiritual, it can be just as spiritually advanced as the others, in fact the earth chakra is essential to give stability to the other chakras.

The earth chakra, the 1st chakra at the base of the spine, is that of Saturn and its two signs: Capricorn, an earth sign, and Aquarius,

Chapter Four

an air sign. The positive characteristics of the earth chakra are steadfastness, determination and loyalty to Truth, which are stable earthy qualities. A negative aspect of earth is excessive rigidity. Saturn can show resistance to change, or stability, depending on whether our response to its energy is negative or positive.

To some degree, the element of the earth chakra describes the more apparent nature of Saturn. Saturn, for example, can feel heavy on our consciousness. However, Saturn can also express the air element of its other sign, Aquarius. Intellect and wisdom are airy characteristics and Saturn can represent the wisdom of detachment. A similar principle is valid for the other chakras: the chakra element describes the more apparent nature of the planet, but the energy of the planet is really a blend of the elements of both its signs.

The 2nd chakra, whose element is water, is that of Jupiter and its signs Sagittarius (fire) and Pisces (water). The consciousness in this chakra is more flowing, expansive and adaptable. Jupiter is the flow of divine grace, but if placed in a difficult position it can mean loss of inspiration and reliance on wrong advice (by flowing with the wrong energy). The reflection off a perfectly still water surface is clear like a mirror: when water is calm it is intuitive, reflecting the inspiration from higher levels of consciousness.

The 3rd chakra, whose element is fire, is that of Mars and its signs Aries (fire) and Scorpio (water). This chakra expresses concentration and direction of energy; energy needs self-control, lest it loses its utility and becomes destructive. Mars is much like a mythical warrior: it can be noble and possessed of mystical prowess in fighting for dharma (righteousness), or be impulsive and submit to anger and destructive, compulsive passions.

The 4th chakra, whose element is air, is that of Venus and its signs Taurus (earth) and Libra (air). The air element represents the expansiveness and sense of kinship with creation we can develop in this chakra, which can manifest as desires, likes and dislikes, or expansive love and devotion. The earthy, more physical side of this chakra manifests in Taurus also as a natural love for things that grow, such as gardens and flowers.

The heart chakra is the seat of chitta, a key concept in yoga.

Planets and chakras

Yogananda describes chitta as consciousness or power of feeling; both reason and feeling have their basis in chitta. Patanjali, the ancient renown yoga teacher, describes yoga as the neutralization of any disturbance in chitta. Yogananda similarly comments: "Transparency to Truth is cultivated by freeing the consciousness, the heart's feeling and the mind's reason, from the dualistic influences of attraction and aversion. Reality cannot be accurately reflected in a consciousness ruffled by likes and dislikes, with their restless passions and desires....But when chitta – human knowing and feeling – is calmed by meditation, the ordinarily agitated ego gives way to the blessed calmness of soul perception."

The 5th chakra, whose element is ether, is that of Mercury and its signs Virgo (earth) and Gemini (air). Ether is subtle, transcending physical reality, and in this chakra our consciousness has the potential to expand and loosen some attachment to ego inclinations and worries. Subtleness requires perception of small differences, and so is accompanied by sensitivity. Subtleness and sensitivity make us receptive to refined states of consciousness, but excessive sensitivity can be uncomfortable or downright difficult, as we become too easily influenced by negative states of mind.

In Mercury's signs we can be subtle in understanding and expressing knowledge. However, if we are not calm, in airy Gemini we can become scattered like the wind, while in earthy Virgo we can be weighted down by worries.

The inner aspect of the ether chakra is dynamic calmness, while the outer aspect is restlessness. By interiorizing and calming our energy, we can develop purity of thought and discrimination. The sanskrit name for this chakra is vishuddha, which means pure.

The last chakra connected to the planets, the 6th chakra, is actually comprised of two poles, one energy center for the Moon and one for the Sun. Moon and its sign Cancer (water) correspond to the pole at the medulla oblongata, in the lower back of the head. The element of this pole is even more subtle than ether, Yogananda called it super-ether. The medulla oblongata is the seat of ego consciousness. Moon is our ego, mind and personality, and Cancer has a very personal view on things.

Sun and its sign Leo (fire) correspond to the pole between the

Chapter Four

eyebrows, the spiritual eye, where in meditation a yogi can see a divine light progressively dissolving the ego to reveal our true nature as the soul.

To remember the connection between planets and chakras, it can be useful to remember that the South Indian notation for writing a chart is in the same order of the chakra progression. Except for the Moon, this is also the same way the planets are ordered in the solar system, by progressive distance to the Sun: the earth chakra is at the base of the spine, and Saturn is the farthest planet from the Sun.

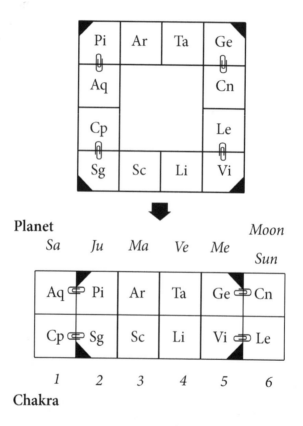

Planets and chakras. The South Indian notation can be collapsed to order the signs in pairs, each corresponding to their chakra and planet.

Chapter Five

Opposite signs

An important concept in astrology is balancing opposite signs. Considering the whole circle of the zodiac is 360 degrees, with 30 degrees for each sign, opposite signs are 180 degrees away from each other, that is the 7th sign counting inclusively from the 1st. Opposite signs have contrasting and complementary characteristics, and balancing them can help us find the best response to their energy.

The sign opposite Aries is Libra. Roughly speaking, Aries is independent and decisive, and may be insensitive in its enthusiasm and focus; Libra is more diplomatic, concerned for others, and idealistic. If out of balance, this pair of signs will express too much of Aries and not enough of Libra, or vice versa. With too much Aries, we might be excessively strong, harsh and focused on ourselves, so it would be better to concentrate on the qualities of Libra and be more diplomatic. If Libra were too strong then we might be too diplomatic and hesitant instead of decisive.

Sometimes, if opposite signs are unbalanced, it may be that one sign is stronger most of the time but occasionally we overcompensate and the opposite becomes too dominant. We might channel a strong and independent Aries, but at times we feel too insensitive and become hesitant at the wrong time, accepting some external influence we should have rather ignored. Or we are normally kind communicators, but in an effort to realize our ideals we become tired of the slow progress of diplomacy and burst out with bossy and uncharacteristic intimations.

Opposite signs are different but also have certain similarities. Aries is the fire sign of Mars and is in the fire chakra; Libra is the air sign of Venus and is in the air chakra. Both fire and air tend to project their energy outward, in contrast to earth and water,

Chapter Five

which are more receptive elements. Fire is willpower and energy, while air is ideas, intellect, knowledge and wisdom; air can also be expansive and sociable.

Aries and Libra, like fire and air, have some things in common and others which are opposite and complementary. Both are dynamic and active signs, but Aries projects the energy of Mars while Libra that of Venus. Mars is the planet of energy and can be very assertive, while Venus is more sensitive and gentle. Venus is the heart chakra, so its position in a chart shows the things we love and desire. Putting together the energies of the air element and of Venus, Libra will be more concerned with ideals rather than pure reason – ideals are a blend of ideas and feelings.

Libra is independent and determined in following its ideals, but it can also be interested in considering how other people will factor in. Aries is very independent, but in contrast to Libra it never seeks anybody's approval or support, and in its willfulness it can run a little hot, like all fire signs.

My family is from Sicily, a fiery island, and people there tend to be quite expressive among friends; if you are not lively they might be concerned you are not feeling too well. I also spent several years in the north of Italy and of Europe where things are a bit cooler; if you are too lively there, they might think you are upset. Our environment can influence our response to the stars and encourage it in one direction or another. Signs and planets, as states of consciousness, can describe not only a person, but also general traits of a group of people. Of all the fire signs Sicilians are closer to Leo than Aries, but they have some of the spontaneous cheerful mood of Aries, and some characteristics of the Sun and of Venus. As another example, Saturn is prominent in England, and together with Mars in Germany.

Aries can be assertive but also undiplomatic; in a confrontation its strength tends to be in your face. The strength of Libra is inside. Libra is the active air sign, so it will actively seek to be true to its ideals and its inner sense of balance. An example of this is Mahatma Gandhi, who fought for India's freedom with non-violence. His Libra ascendant draws strength from both Venus and Mars: a peaceful warrior.

Opposite signs

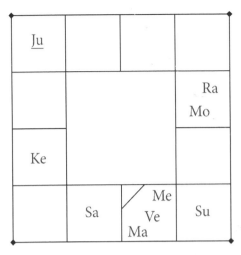

Chart of Mahatma Gandhi. The diagonal line in Libra is the symbol for the ascendant. Libra has strength because its ruler, Venus, is in own sign.

This is an example of how planets can blend their energies: Venus is strong in its own sign, showing the depth of commitment to his ideals of freedom and sacredness of all life; Mars shows the strength to fight for them even at the cost of his life.

Energetically, Venus here gives strength to Mars because planets blend their energies when they are either in the same or opposite sign. Whether this mutual influence is supportive or overbearing depends on whether we are able to balance the two energies or not. The strength of a sign or a planet does not guarantee that we are expressing its energy in a positive way, but it is good to have energy if we know how to use it correctly!

Libra's inclination to be concerned for others is a balancing influence for a strong Aries. If brought to excess, though, this inclination might result in a difficulty to stand up for oneself.

Mahatma Gandhi displayed enormous courage in his fight for freedom and strict application of ahimsa, non-violence. Gandhi's concept of non-violence was extreme: he did not condone physical action for any reason, even in defence of innocents in need of immediate protection. Yogananda had great love and respect for Gandhi, however he noted that, in such cases, the dharmic course

Chapter Five

of action would be to protect the innocents, even causing physical harm to the attacker if unavoidable. In such an extreme situation, however, it would be important to preserve a non-violent frame of mind, and not feel any hatred against the attacker.

In the chart of Gandhi Libra is strong, and Mars shares some of this strength, representing his admirable courage. However, Mars in Libra is not as strong as Mars would be in Aries. In this chart Libra is stronger than Aries, so there is a subtle imbalance, which helps us understand Gandhi's interpretation of ahimsa.

In any chart where Aries is weak, for example because Mars is in a difficult sign, we should consciously seek to develop self-confidence and assertiveness. This does not mean forgetting our gentle Libran nature, but rather finding inner balance; strength is needed to be true to our ideals.

But more than strength is needed: as Kriyananda notes, the deeper motivation of Libra is inner harmony; its inclination to take into consideration the needs of others will remain superficial if not expanded into unselfishness.

Ke			Mo
			Sa
Ma			Ve
		Me Ju	Su Ra

Chart of Lahiri Mahasaya. The ascendant is Libra and Venus, its ruler, is in Leo. The highest expression of Leo is to shine an inspiring light for the benefit of others.

A yoga master with strong Libra was Lahiri Mahasaya. Throughout his life he exemplified the perfect inner balance between meditation and world involvement: an accountant and householder by day, at night he would sit in meditation and teach his disciples. He also had a very strong Mars, whose energy he used to reintroduce to the public world the meditation technique of Kriya Yoga.

Both Lahiri Mahasaya and Sri Yukteswar display a perfect balance of Libra and Aries: the inner strength of uncompromising principles, and kindness in helping others find freedom and happiness.

However they had different external personalities, one emphasising Aries, and the other Libra. Sri Yukteswar would not work as a dependent to anybody, and though gentle to all visitors, his teaching methods for his few close disciples "cannot be described as other than drastic", in the words of Yogananda. Lahiri Mahasaya, on the other hand, was an accountant working for the government, and had a vast number of disciples. These apparent differences are reflected in their charts, as masters choose the time of their birth according to their mission, however they were both one with God in their true inner consciousness. The same is true for us as well, we only need to remember it – we have a chart, we are not our chart.

To continue with the concept of balancing opposite signs, lets consider the other two signs of Mars and Venus, Scorpio and Taurus, which are also opposite each other – not surprisingly, since Mars and Venus have complementary qualities. Taurus is the fixed earth sign, while Scorpio is fixed water. Being fixed, both are focused on the characteristics of their elements, whether in an attentive or excessive way.

Earth is practical, steady, determined, and it represents form. A strong Taurus can give greatly sustaining energy to anything we do; it is a Venus sign, gentle and with love for beauty. A spiritually immature response to its influence would be excessive concern for material possessions, self-doubt and immovability. This happens if we look for security and happiness in external sources, be them

Chapter Five

tangible physical objects, or more abstract, but still seemingly dependable, organized plans and ideas. In this case we would do well to learn to be more changeable and adaptable like the flowing water of Scorpio.

Scorpio seeks depth of understanding, consciousness and happiness. In contrast to Taurus, Scorpio is inclined to look for them inside. If we do the same in Taurus, we will become fixed in the subtler inner qualities of earth: steadfastness and loyalty to Truth.

Conversely, Scorpio can be excessively intense in its feelings and emotions, if the passion and energy of Mars are out of control. Scorpio can then become self-destructive in pursuit of temporary sense happiness. The gentle earthy calmness of Taurus is shunned by an immature Scorpio, but it is a balm to the exhausted or spiritually advanced Scorpio.

The difference between Taurus and Scorpio is made even clearer by their interaction with the Moon. The changeable Moon, which represents our personal nature, mind, emotions and feelings, is in a challenging position in Scorpio because we tend to respond to this combination with excessive emotional sensitivity. The stability of Taurus and its naturally agreeable sociable nature can be a calming influence for unsettling emotions. Then Moon in Scorpio, combined with the calmness and stability of the opposite sign, will give perceptive insight and an ability to give counsel. On the other hand, the Moon in the sign of Taurus is naturally supportive and shows a determined mind. The astrological shorthand is to say the Moon is exalted in Taurus and debilitated in Scorpio.

Each planet is exalted in a specific sign and debilitated in the sign opposite. It is generally good to have a planet exalted, as it will be strong energetically. In some cases, an exalted planet might not be the most favorably placed in a chart, by other factors, however exaltation still shows an easier possibility of developing the highest expression of that planet. It is not nice to hear a planet is debilitated in your chart, however it is just indicating a specific lesson that we need to learn, and once it is learnt, we will unlock its good qualities. The perceptive advice we can receive from a friend with Moon in Scorpio is possible because they have successfully overcome a similar problem in the past.

Studying the exaltation and debilitation of the Moon is helpful in understanding Taurus and Scorpio. Similarly, we can learn about other signs and planets by understanding why they are stronger in some combinations and not in others. Moon is strongest in Taurus where it is exalted; it is also strong in its own sign, Cancer. Planets are stronger in their exaltation sign rather than in the sign they rule, but it's not a huge difference.

Cancer, the sign of the Moon, is opposite Capricorn, a sign of Saturn. These are the next pair of opposite signs that we will study. Jupiter is exalted in Cancer and debilitated in Capricorn.

A positive example of a master with debilitated Jupiter is Satya Sai Baba, who received millions of dollars in donations for his charitable work in building hospitals and schools for the poor, in India. In his chart Jupiter, the planet of expansion, generosity and spiritual aspirations, is in Capricorn which is a sign of Saturn. Where Jupiter is expansion, Saturn is contraction. Contraction can be good if it denotes concentration and focus on something positive. If our response to Saturn's energy is not perfect, though, we can feel it as the most difficult of all planets, as it is the most strict in teaching its lessons. We may then experience it as a general sense of heaviness, self-doubt or downright fear and suffering. These negative feelings make us contract into selfishness.

The element of Saturn's chakra is earth, and earth signs in general can be vulnerable to feelings of insecurity until we learn that our happiness does not rely on anything set in form. Joy is ours already, we need but remember it.

When facing any difficulty brought by our response to Saturn, it is useful to remember that help is always only a step away. The deepest reason and purpose of any difficulty is always spiritual. An honest effort in understanding our shortcomings will immediately give some relief. By battling to overcome any obstacle we do become stronger; by responding to Saturn's energy in a good way,

Chapter Five

this planet will greatly support us on the spiritual path.

Capricorn is the active earth sign, it has great power in methodically pursuing practical projects and developing concentration, however an imperfect response can show skepticism and excessive doubts. In this sense Jupiter is not immediately at ease in this sign and it can lose its inspiration and creativity. I have Jupiter in Capricorn and I experience this first hand: if I don't sustain my energy at a higher level I lose my intuition and make the wrong choice, usually because I worry too much about being realistic.

But as Kriyananda says about Capricorn, it is important to ask yourself if you are really being realistic. If our sense of reality is based on beliefs rather than on experienced truth, eventually our mind becomes mired in dogmas or skepticism. In fact, a typical immature response to Saturn's energy is holding onto a traditionalist or conservative mindset, resistant to change.

Jupiter is then said to be debilitated in Capricorn, but the mature expression of this combination is rather that Jupiter's spiritual aspirations, generosity and creativity will be steadily developed in a practical way. They will also likely express on a practical, earthy, level, just like the charitable work of Satya Sai Baba.

One way I try to express practical generosity is cooking for my friends; my first tries were pitiful, but by methodical practice (Capricorn and Saturn) I learnt to prepare edible food. Good food is important in Sicily and when I was a child I'd see my grandmother or mother cook and I saw it as a sign of love, so I do it as a gesture of affection.

The impersonal Saturn traits of Capricorn are opposite the very personal Cancer. The Moon sign is associated with the medulla oblongata, the seat of the ego, ahamkara. Swamiji explains about the ego: upon seeing a horse, the intellect (buddhi) recognizes it as a concept; the ego will then add "this is *my* horse!" This is the deeply personal focus of Cancer.

Both Capricorn and Cancer can manifest positive and negative traits of concentration, depending whether they are spiritually expansive or selfishly contracting. Cancer is active water and its focus is strongly colored by feelings. If our response to Cancer's

Opposite signs

energy is selfish, we can be insensitive towards others, while at the same time oversensitive regarding anything perceived as disagreeable to us. We can respond in an expansive way to Cancer's focus by gradually realizing that it is not just about *ourselves, our* family, *our* friends, or *our* country, but that God is in everyone, so everyone is our own.

If we are expansive, the earthy stability and impersonal detachment of Capricorn can then help us achieve, in Cancer, the calm intuition and empathy of which all water signs are capable.

An expansive Cancer is innately warm and caring, in turn a good balance for Capricorn. Impersonal wisdom and personal compassion cannot truly be expressed without possessing the other. Yogananda said: "It is foolish to say that God is not personal. God is very personal, he has become all of us!"

Jupiter's sanskrit name is Guru, because this planet is a spiritual teacher who expands our ego; it is exalted in Cancer, whose gentle focalising power balances the planet's expansiveness. By contrast, Saturn's concentrating power is starker and not immediately harmonious. Cancer, as a water sign ruled by the Moon, represents our mind's receptivity to Jupiter's expansive influence. Jupiter represents the prosperity received through divine grace; to be receptive to grace we need expansive awareness and sensitivity to flow with its energy. Prosperity is attracted by generosity. The sensitive and caring water qualities of Cancer are inclined to flow with Jupiter's energy, while the practical and realistic attitude of Capricorn can bring doubts.

In the words of Yogananda: "There are two kinds of doubt: destructive and constructive. Destructive doubt is habitual skepticism. People who cultivate this attitude are as blind in their disbelief as any bigot in his bigotry. For such people, impartial investigation has no relevance. They want only that information which will negate new ideas, and which agrees with their own, or with the prevailing, opinions. Skepticism is like static in the radio of the mind. It prevents a person from receiving the broadcasts of intuition from the silence within. Constructive doubt, on the other hand, is intelligent questioning, and fair, impartial examination. Those who cultivate this attitude never prejudge an idea. Nor

Chapter Five

do they accept as valid the unsubstantiated opinions of others. They keep an open mind, and base their conclusions on objective tests. They seek above all to verify those conclusions by their own experience. This is the proper approach to truth."

Destructive doubts stop the flow of divine grace; constructive doubts do not. To understand the lesson of Jupiter in Capricorn we need to learn the difference. The constructive doubts and objectivity of Capricorn are helpful in balancing Cancer, which otherwise can be lost in excessive focus on subjective feelings.

What we understand about balancing Capricorn and Cancer can help us interpret any other combination of their rulers, for example if Saturn and Moon are in the same sign. Moon is our mind and feelings, and any tint of selfishness and excessive emotionality can provoke a sense of unhappiness and heaviness from Saturn. While this can be true, in general, about Saturn's influence in any chart, it is particularly true if there is a specific connection with the Moon. Only by actively looking for a balance of personal and impersonal views will we unlock the spiritual energy of Moon and Saturn. Saturn then gives equanimity and strong inner peace.

In general Saturn is positioned in a chart where we have excessively dwelt in the past. For example, if we have Saturn in Leo, in a past life we might have focused on Leo's traits in a not entirely positive way – maybe we were too proud and authoritative. By progressing on the spiritual path we find the right attitude to respond to Saturn, which is to be unselfish and do our best without expectations for the results of our actions.

Saturn is exalted in Libra, in the heart chakra: the gentle loving energy of Venus can balance the impersonal detachment of Saturn. Libra is an air sign, more detached and not as personal as other soft signs like watery Cancer, thus it is easier to harmonize with impersonal Saturn.

On the other hand Saturn is not immediately strong in Aries, as it is slow and methodical, while Aries is quick and passionate. If

Opposite signs

not understood and resolved, this contrast can result in impatience, frustration and hesitation, and actions that are rushed without deliberate concentration.

Mars in a Saturn sign, however, is a naturally supporting combination: Mars is strong in Capricorn, its sign of exaltation. The planet of energy benefits from Saturn's discipline, with the potential of achieving perfect control, just like Lahiri Mahasaya who had Mars exalted.

Drupada said one of the highest traits of Mars is penetrating insight, and finding knowledge through enquiry, understanding how things work, so it is associated with engineering and techniques in general. In the case of Lahiri Mahasaya, Mars signified the reintroduction of the technique of Kriya Yoga to anyone with a sincere interest, instead of only the monastic caste of India, the Swamis.

Chapter Six

Planets and yoga

An ancient treatise on yoga written by Patanjali, the Yoga Sutras, describes a few concepts essential for a yogi. Yogananda and Kriyananda have explained how each of these concepts is connected to each planet and its chakra.

The 1st concept is yama, the powers of mental resistance: non-violence, non-lying, non-avarice, non-sensuality and non-attachment. If we lack, or have lacked in the past, in mental resistance, we will encounter obstacles and difficulties, manifested by Saturn. When necessary, Saturn seeks to limit our negativity by making tangible the consequences of our actions; sometimes we are not aware of the necessity to change until we slam onto a wall. Yama means control and it is contractive like Saturn; the earth chakra is that of yama, Saturn, Capricorn and Aquarius.

The 2nd concept is niyama, the powers of mental adherence: cleanliness, contentment, austerity, introspection, and spiritual devotion. These are characteristics of Jupiter, planet of wisdom, spiritual enthusiasm and devotion. Niyama means non-control and it is expansive like Jupiter; theirs is the water chakra.

The 3rd concept is asana, self-control, both in mind and body. Mars, the fiery planet of energy and action, especially benefits from self-control and spiritual discipline. Asana means posture, such as that needed in meditation; to hold a good comfortable posture we must be physically still and mentally calm. Like Mars, asana relates to the fire chakra.

Fire is willpower and energy, so we might respond to its strength with a desire to direct it with effort at all times. To perfect asana we need to balance effort and control, willpower and relaxed surrender. Not trying enough is laziness, but trying too hard is the same as not listening to inner guidance. Trying too hard

Planets and yoga

means putting a lot of energy into motion without the proper sensitivity to direct it.

If a chart shows an obstacle for Mars (like being in debilitation) or its signs (like Saturn in Aries), it could indicate a difficulty in being energetic or taking decisive action to start anew; it could also indicate impulsiveness. Without control we will act without thought, or fail to act at the right time. Self-control is something we all would do well to learn, however the importance of this quality is emphasized with Mars and its signs.

The 4th concept is pranayama; yama means control and prana is life-energy, breath, air. Its chakra is that of Venus, the air chakra. Venus is our heart, the center of our likes and dislikes. With pranayama we control our desires and life-energy, abandoning the temporary happiness of the senses to remember divine joy. Pranayama is best achieved through meditation techniques. Ultimately, we need to be able to control our energy perfectly, much as Lahiri Mahasaya, who would often sit all night silently in samadhi, surrounded by his disciples.

The 5th concept is pratyahara, interiorization of the mind, which brings mental calmness. It corresponds to the ether chakra, like Mercury, the planet of perception. Ether forms the boundary between the physical world and the subtle inner worlds. If we are caught up by our outward life we become restless. By withdrawing our attention from the physical world, we transcend it much like the ether element.

Control and interiorization of prana (yama, pranayama and pratyahara) are all closely related: it is not a coincidence that the three air (prana) signs are ruled by Saturn (yama), Venus (pranayama) and Mercury (pratyahara).

The last three concepts are often grouped together: they are dharana, concentration; dhyana, meditation; and samadhi, divine union. In these final steps of yoga we stop identifying with the ego (Moon and medulla oblongata) and start remembering we are the soul (Sun and spiritual eye).

Chapter Seven

Planets and houses

The ascendant is normally the starting point in interpreting a chart as it is its root. It indicates some of the same characteristics of the Sun: vitality, self-expression and confidence. The sign of the ascendant is also called the 1st house; the next sign going clockwise is the 2nd house, and so on forming twelve houses. Each house has specific meanings, for example the 5th house is creativity, while the 7th house is relationships, both romantic and not. Houses are states of our consciousness focused on specific experiences. Each house falls in one sign, which will specifically influence the meanings of that house. By combining houses, signs and planets we can do most chart interpretations. The sanskrit word for an astrological house is bhava, one meaning being attitude of the mind. This translation highlights the fact that the houses describe, first and foremost, the state of mind with which we relate to that specific area of our life; our mental attitude then attracts good and bad experiences depending on our energetic habits from the past, and the present application of willpower.

Each of the twelve ascendants places the houses in different signs. For Aries ascendants the 2nd house is Taurus and the 9th house is Sagittarius, while for Scorpio ascendants the 9th house is Cancer. The 9th is a house of spirituality. Speaking in general terms, a Scorpio ascendant is inclined to feel its spirituality through Cancer qualities: very personal and focused on feelings. For Leo ascendants the 9th house is Aries: they are inclined at first to be independent and willful in their spiritual aspirations. However, developing our spirituality makes us less influenced by the stars. Being born with an ascendant does not set our life in stone, nor our spiritual aspirations remain bound by the sign where the 9th house falls. That sign is a starting point from where we can

Planets and houses

expand; the same is true for all houses.

For a more specific example on how to read houses, lets look at *Anne's chart: the ascendant is Libra, ruled by Venus. A general principle in astrology is that a special relationship exists between a planet and its signs: no matter where they are placed, their energy and strength are always connected. As a consequence, to understand an ascendant we also have to look at its ruler; Venus in this chart is then especially important.

Jupiter and Venus are the most benefic planets in general, and in this chart both are in water signs, a sensitive element: Anne is generous and concerned for others.

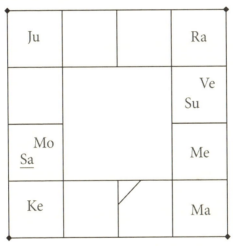

Anne's chart. Venus in Cancer draws strength from being in the 10th house, a strong house. Venus and Cancer also receive some strength from the Moon: any planet opposite its own sign gives it strength.

Venus is in the 10th house of career and public action. Jupiter is in the 6th house of obstacles and overcoming obstacles, like health problems and healing. To overcome an obstacle we often need a practical way or method, so the 6th is a practical house. It is also the house of service to others (removing their obstacles) and karma yoga, that is yoga through action and seeing every action as service to God. By profession Anne practices and teaches different energy-healing techniques.

Chapter Seven

The energy confluence in the chart is threefold:

1. Venus, the ascendant ruler, is in the 10th house, so public work is a primary focus for Anne;

2. expansive Jupiter supports Venus, as both are in water signs, showing sensitivity to the difficulties of others;

3. Jupiter rules the 3rd house of motivation and the 6th house of karma yoga, so Anne will likely be interested and motivated in a job which is expansive and helpful.

We have combined three concepts: houses, signs and planets. The houses, which are directly connected to the planets we are considering, are the 10th house for Venus and the 3rd and 6th house for Jupiter; these give a specific focus: work, motivation, and practical healing techniques. The signs, Cancer and Pisces, are both water with a focus on feelings and sensitivity. The general qualities of the planets, Jupiter and Venus, are benefic: Jupiter is expansive, generous and naturally oriented to wisdom, Venus is sensitive and searching for happiness; in this case Venus rules the ascendant making it especially positive.

This combination of energy was created by Anne's efforts and it shows her past karma, her energetic habits formed in the past. The stars are a mirror of her aura. By her own free will, in this lifetime she has chosen to respond to these inclinations by dedicating her work to helping others. In fact, she hasn't always been a healer, she was working in a commercial business before taking this decision. Her chart was the same when she had a more materially oriented career.

Other planets which influence Anne's Venus are the Sun, which is also in Cancer, and Saturn and Moon, which are directly opposite in Capricorn. Planets in the same sign will mix their energies, but also planets in opposite signs are in direct communication. These four planets will all influence each other but the strongest is Saturn as it is in own sign. Since Saturn can be a bit overbearing, we should be careful of the shadows it can cast on the other three planets, especially the Moon. What matters is our response to Saturn's energy. In earthy Capricorn it is important to not respond to Saturn's strength by becoming excessively detached and impersonal, too resistant to change and to listening. True detachment is a spiritual accomplishment but it should increase, not decrease, our kindness – otherwise we are just being too cold and unsympathetic.

Saturn can also be a wisdom guide for the other three planets, preventing them from going the wrong way. For example, the Sun enjoys being visible in the 10th house of status and fame, which could make us proud; Saturn, a contractive influence, is likely to prevent that, in fact Anne is rather humble.

The 10th house is the most visible house because it corresponds to the top of the sky; the ascendant is the eastern horizon, the 7th house is the west, the 4th house is hidden underneath the earth. The 10th house is midday, the 4th house midnight. Just like opposite signs, opposite houses have complementary qualities. The 10th house is more prominent and publicly visible. The 4th house is opposite, so it is a house of things that are more intimate and instrumental to our inner state of being: inner happiness, home, and mother, whether human or Divine.

The Sun, in Anne's chart, rules the 11th house of public family and community: the 10th and 11th houses blend, a confirmation that her career is directly related to community. The Sun is the most visible planet in the sky, and it is visible in the 10th house; this shows some visibility in her profession, as she teaches in different centers and even abroad.

Another thing to notice is that Mars is in the 12th house. This is a house of spirituality, but it is also called the house of loss, for we might have a material loss for a spiritual gain. Energetically, it is not a strong house, it is where we lose identification with our ego to acquire an awareness that is more universal. In other words, it is a house of dissolution, whether it dissolves our sense of identification with the ego, or our possessions.

Mars in the 12th house for a Libra ascendant requires a strong

Chapter Seven

dedication to spiritual wisdom to avoid being easily swayed by others when a decisive action needs to be taken. The reason is that Libra's energy needs to be balanced with that of Aries; if Mars is weak and Aries is not supported by other planets it can indicate a lack of decisiveness. Virgo is a thinking sign, while Mars is the planet of action, so in Virgo it might become hesitant, thinking too much instead of acting. It could also be discouraged by criticism; it is not a naturally harmonious placement for most people. If, however, we learn to respond correctly to this energy, we have the planet of energy in a thinking sign: we learn to act with discrimination.

Virgo is the mutable earth sign of Mercury. Active signs are related to the creative principle of Brahma, and fixed signs to the preserving and sustaining principle of Vishnu. Mutable signs have the qualities of Shiva. Brahma is the creative aspect of God, then Vishnu sustains the existence of the universe after creation, until Shiva dissolves it back into Spirit.

Drupada said mutable signs represent the point where, having started and sustained an experience, we extract its essence and let it go, dissolving it to prepare for the next. Such a step, when done with discernment, requires subtlety: the sensitivity of perception of mutable signs is both their strength and weakness.

Virgo is mutable earth, so it is most sensitive to material environment and form, and can indicate allergies or health issues in general. However Mercury represents our intellect, and its chakra is ether (transcending form), which makes Virgo somewhat airy in character even though its element is earth. Earth is more tied to form, while air to pure ideas, so Virgo is especially related to applied knowledge and techniques. Pratyahara, interiorization of life-energy, is the yoga concept for the chakra of Mercury: a positive response to a strong Virgo can give great calmness, wisdom and discrimination.

If there is some difficulty related to Virgo we should be careful not to overanalyze or criticize, or be too sensitive of perceived criticism. Special efforts to protect our physical health would also be a good idea. A potentially difficult placement affecting Virgo is Mercury debilitated in Pisces, because signs and their ruler

Planets and houses

are always connected, and opposite signs talk to each other. It follows that Mercury is strong (exalted) when in Virgo, giving an inclination to develop a discriminative intellect. This is the only case of a planet being exalted in its own sign.

Mercury has a quick and young energy, it is the smallest planet and closest to the Sun, taking only about three months to complete one rotation around our star. The only other planet closer than Earth is Venus. As a consequence of their inner orbit, in a chart Mercury can be at most one sign away from the Sun, while Venus one and a half.

In a way, we can look at the two signs of Mercury, airy Gemini and earthy Virgo, as being shades of ether, the element of their chakra. Both signs are inclined to transcend form and have the subtlety of mutable signs. Mercury is strong in Gemini, however it can also be restless, while the earthy stability and receptivity of Virgo make it its sign of exaltation. Yogananda said: "True discrimination does not come through a process of logical reasoning, but as a revelation from within. It is born of calm meditation and divine contact." Discrimination is achieved with insight and intuition: it requires a balance between Virgo and its opposite sign, Pisces.

Pisces is mutable water, softer than fiery or airy signs, as water and earth are more receptive than projecting. Softer does not mean weaker though, but merely inclined to give a perceptive and expansive sensitivity. By contrast Gemini, mutable air, is more sensitive to ideas.

The perceptive sensitivity of water is expressed differently depending on the modality of the sign. In fixed Scorpio its direction is deeper inward in intensity, while Cancer can be dynamically active in expressing it with a personal focus. Pisces is expansive, being a sign of Jupiter, and as a mutable sign it can be very sensitive to its emotional environment; its direction is dissolving (like Shiva) outward.

Virgo is the sign of focus and discrimination, Pisces that of insight and intuition. Excessive focus prevents insight, because it gives too much attention to details without ever looking at the whole. However, lack of focus results in excessive openness and a consciousness that picks up influences subconsciously, like a

Chapter Seven

sponge. Pisces needs a strong center, because its natural capacity for universal empathy can become a tendency to be too easily swayed by other people's feelings.

Both signs of Mercury are opposite the signs of Jupiter: the expansivity of Jupiter needs to be checked by common sense and reason, until it is firmly grounded in intuition. Excessive reliance on reason, however, prevents the actual development of wisdom, and of trust in seemingly intangible but uplifting feelings. Because of its expansive watery qualities, Pisces is the sign of compassion and devotion.

Chapter Eight

Signs and houses

There is a natural affinity between the houses and the signs of the natural zodiac, the zodiac starting from Aries: the 1st house with Aries, the 2nd house with Taurus, and so on. The 1st house represents self, our strength, self-confidence and vitality; these are also indicated by a strong Aries, with its ability to trace its path even against strong opposition. The 7th house is relationships, that which is opposite to us, that mirrors or complements us, and Libra is naturally more aware than Aries of its social connections, and the need to find one's inner balance. The 12th house indicates spirituality, renunciation and the expansion and dissolution of the ego; Pisces gives an inclination to universal empathy, and to not put oneself in the forefront, which can lead to the meanings of the 12th house.

The expansive qualities of the 12th house are complemented by the attention to details of Virgo and the 6th house, where we develop discrimination. Opposite houses like the 6th and 12th have complementary qualities, similarly to opposite signs: we've already seen the 1st and 7th, and the 4th (home, inner happiness) and 10th (work, public life, status).

The 6th house is not energetically strong because it represents learning, when we face practical difficulties and obstacles and become stronger in the process. To do this successfully, we need to be attentive like Virgo! It is also the house of service to others, as we help them overcome their difficulties. It is a house where we go through a transition, a learning process. The yoga concept for Virgo is pratyahara, the calmness given by interiorization; similarly, a strong 6th house can give calmness in confronting obstacles using discrimination. Probably not at first, as the 6th house indicates challenges, but it is a definite potential.

Chapter Eight

As a last example, another house of spirituality is the 9th, but where the 12th is the house of renunciation and liberation, the 9th is that of prosperity and divine grace. Sagittarius is the 9th sign of the natural zodiac so it has an affinity with the 9th house. The keywords Kriyananda gives for Sagittarius are upward aspiration and searching for universal awareness, 9th house meanings. The highest expression of Sagittarius is joyful and enthusiastic. These words from Yogananda describe the best mood of Sagittarius: "True happiness is not the fruit of years of painful struggle and anxiety. It is a long succession, rather, of little decisions simply to be happy in the moment."

The reason of the affinity between signs and houses is that the signs form a pattern of energy, defined by their basic characteristics and elements. This pattern begins with the creative energy of Aries, active fire, transitions to the stable fixed earth of Taurus, and continues throughout the twelve signs, completing the circle with Pisces, whose mutable water symbolizes the dissolution of the ego back into Infinity.

The basic pattern of this circle of energy is echoed in other things, for example the seasons. Kriyananda describes how each of the four seasons is comprised of three signs. Aries symbolizes the youthful beginning of a new spring, which continues in the eager spurts of growth of Taurus, the sign of mid spring, and goes on through summer, fall and winter, closing with Pisces, the last sign of winter – only to begin again with a new spring.

This link between seasons and signs is the basis of Western astrology, so called because it is currently the most known in the West. Kriyananda aptly calls it solar astrology, because it connects Aries, the sign of beginnings, to the beginning of spring. Spring itself is the beginning of the year for the Sun, the time when it starts shining longer and stronger.

The cycle of the seasons depends only on the relative orientation of the Sun and Earth, it does not depend in any way on the stars. What can be confusing is that Western astrologers use the names of the real star-signs to refer to the twelve divisions of the seasons. They consider the Sun as being in Aries at the beginning of spring, however in reality at that time the Sun is not in Aries,

Signs and houses

it is actually in the stars of Pisces. What is true is that the Sun is at the beginning of the four seasons, a time with some Aries qualities. About fifteen hundred years ago, the Sun was in the constellation of Aries at the beginning of spring, and in about five hundred years from now it will be in Aquarius. The reason is that the solar system is slowly moving relative to the zodiac.

Solar astrology is not directly based on the real star-signs and the constellations that we can see in the sky, but on the affinity between the seasons and the pattern of energy formed by the circle of the twelve real signs. Astrology directly based on the star-signs, as described in this book, is often called Vedic astrology, taking its name from the Vedas, the ancient sacred texts of India where it is described; its real name is Jyotish, which means the science of light. Kriyananda discusses further the difference between solar astrology and Jyotish in his book *The Sun Sign as a Spiritual Guide*.

To summarize, the pattern of energy described by the real signs is echoed in the seasons, but each of the twelve divisions of the seasons is confusingly called with the same name of a real sign. Because the seasons are based on the Earth's orbit in the solar system, rather than the far away stars, they form a more local point of view. Reading a chart based on the seasons may be more appropriate if we are interested only on the surface of our consciousness. I do not mean this point of view is superficial in a negative sense, but it is more restricted to our personality, orbiting around the local light of the personal interests of our ego. Obviously a yogi has a personality, but is trying to transcend it.

In any case, the energy pattern formed by the signs is real and visible in the seasons as well – it also exists in a chart as the twelve houses. The difference lies in the point taken as the beginning. Aries is the sign of beginnings. For the seasons, the beginning is spring, while for a chart it is the ascendant, the direction of the rising Sun at the time of our birth.

By extension, the ascendant represents the birth of each moment, so we can cast a chart at any moment which represents a beginning. If a group of people comes together to start a project, a chart for that moment will describe the energy of the group and of the project. Some astrologers in India cast a chart for the exact time

Chapter Eight

when someone asks them a question, and the chart will describe the energy and answer for that question.

Since the pattern of twelve houses parallels that of the twelve signs, the houses naturally follow the same sequence of elements of the signs: fire, earth, air, water. Just like Aries, the 1st house has a fire quality to it: energy and willpower is needed for new beginnings. However, a more specific way to describe the houses is by using four concepts, whose characteristics are based on the four elements: dharma, artha, kama and moksha. Dharma is righteousness, artha is practical resources, kama is motivation and desires, moksha is happiness and liberation. The element of dharma is fire, that of artha is earth, kama is air and moksha is water.

Understanding the four house kinds is useful when learning about the meanings of the houses, in the same way as we can understand signs by their element. Artha, kama and moksha are perhaps more straightforward to understand, at least on a basic level. Dharma is doing what's right, relative to the situation we are in: Kriyananda explains how for a lazy person it would be dharmic to decide to work hard at improving even only his material conditions, but for a saintly person devoted to humanitarian service it would not be dharmic to forget their spiritual call and look exclusively for material riches. It is dharmic to always say the truth, but if saying the truth would endanger the life of an innocent person, then it would be dharmic not to say it. This does not mean that dharma is relative: dharma is always a way to expand our consciousness and be closer to God. To follow dharma we need wisdom.

Chapter Nine

Groups of houses

The sequence of dharma, artha, kama and moksha is repeated three times in the twelve houses: the 1st house is dharma, the 2nd artha, and so on. There are then three dharma houses (1st, 5th and 9th), and three of each other kind.

12 moksha	1 dharma	2 artha	3 kama
11 kama			4 moksha
10 artha			5 dharma
9 dharma	8 moksha	7 kama	6 artha

Houses for Aries ascendants. The 1st house, the ascendant, is always a dharma house. The other houses and their kind follow in a clockwise sequence. Each house kind corresponds to an element: dharma is fire. When the ascendant is in Aries, a fire sign, the element of each house is the same of the element of the sign it falls in: a good way to memorize house kinds if you know the element of the signs.

The immediate focus of the first dharma house is more personal, that of the second dharma house is relating to others, while that of the third dharma house is on a larger and more impersonal reality.

Chapter Nine

The same is true for the other three groups of house kinds: the first house of each kind has a personal view, the second relational, and the third universal.

Since the first four houses from the ascendant are each the first of their kind, they have a more personal point of view, the middle four generally focus on how we relate to others, and the last four on how we connect to wider realities. This is only a broad categorization.

Rather than describe the twelve houses going around in order, we can divide them by their kind in four groups. The first group is that of dharma houses. Dharma is what takes us closer to God. We need strength of will to follow our dharma in the face of inner and outer opposition, and the element of dharma houses is fire. These are the 1st, 5th and 9th houses and they are the most benefic houses, especially the 9th, which is the house of prosperity, divine grace and spirituality. The planets which rule these houses in a chart are especially benevolent; even Saturn loses much of its difficult energy when ruling a dharma house.

Another reason of the supportive nature of the dharma houses is that signs of the same element are harmonious, and the 5th and 9th signs are always of the same element of the ascendant.

Keeping in mind the affinity between houses and the natural zodiac, Aries and the 1st house represent the willpower to follow our dharma; Leo and the 5th house the established intelligence, creativity and good karma from past adherence to dharma, as well as the desire to share it with others; Sagittarius and the 9th house our aspiration to reach Spirit. Sagittarius is the mutable fire sign, so it aptly represents the highest fruition of following dharma – mutable signs reach for the essence of their element. Sagittarius is an expansive Jupiter sign with a great capacity for enthusiasm, as it seeks to reconnect us with our true nature, divine joy.

In my chart (on page 79) I have two strong dharma houses, the 1st and the 9th. My ascendant is Leo, its ruler, the Sun, is in Aries, exalted in the 9th house, with Mercury. My 9th house is obviously strong, but the ascendant also has strength, because of the connection between Sun and its sign Leo. Mercury also shares the strength of the Sun by occupying the same sign. Mercury, our intellect and awareness, is made bright by the light of the Sun, as long as it is not too close: any planet within a few degrees of the Sun is called combust.

Combustion enhances the spiritual inner traits of a planet, but it can affect the outer meanings. A combust Mercury could indicate a capacity for bright insight, but also nervous restlessness. Perhaps, similarly to Mercury in Pisces, also occasional forgetfulness or inattentiveness if our intellect becomes burnt out.

The effects of combustion are entirely dependent on our response to the extra energy: the combust planet receives a greater amount of light from the Sun, how much of it can we manage? Sri Yukteswar had Mercury very close to the Sun, technically combust, but the bright intellect of a master is capable of withstanding the full light of the Sun. It follows that, if we make an effort, the negative indications of combustion, much like debilitation, will be overcome to a progressively higher degree. As a rule of thumb, I personally consider 5 degrees as the distance from the Sun at which combustion effects might be worth mentioning, for all planets.

The strength of my 9th house shows in a few things: I have a PhD in Physics from the University of Cambridge, and a Self-realized guru, Paramhansa Yogananda. Sun and Mercury in Aries also show independent thinking. On the other hand, it took me a long time to start learning to listen and receive, and to not get into occasional but heated and impulsive arguments. The Sun is willpower, and a willful person often does not like to be told what to do. Similarly, Mercury represents communication and it can be too hot in the fiery Mars sign.

Apart Aries, my Taurus is also reasonably strong with Venus in own sign, though Venus is within the very 1st degree so it doesn't have full strength, as it is just entering the sign. However, it is my 10th house, which in general is the strongest house. The strongest houses in any chart are, in increasing order, the 1st, 4th, 7th and 10th; these angular houses give energy to any planet which occupies them.

The reason is that the 1st, 4th, 7th and 10th signs of the natural zodiac are all active in modality, so they are energetic, ready to act; each is of a different element, and together they represent the active interaction of fire, water, air and earth. Because the houses are based on the pattern of energy of the signs, the four angular houses retain the active strength of those four signs.

Drawing the twelve houses in a circle, the angular houses form a square with one angular house in each corner, while the dharma houses form an equilateral triangle, so they are called trine houses.

In my chart, Taurus, Venus and Saturn receive strength by being in the 10th house. Between the strength of Aries and Taurus, I am rather stubborn! It has taken great effort for me to start turning my stubbornness into inner stability, and all my effort would have been in vain if not for the grace of my guru.

The dharma houses are the most auspicious, so if their rulers are strong it is a blessing, especially if one of them is Jupiter or Venus, which have the most benefic temperament. For example, for Aries ascendant the 9th ruler is Jupiter. Jupiter would be strong in the 9th house, in its own sign of Sagittarius, or exalted in Cancer, in the 4th house. In the 5th house, in Leo, it would also be good. By contrast, if the Sun, the 5th ruler for Aries ascendant, were in Aries, exalted, then we should keep in mind that the Sun is not as gentle as Jupiter: as a dharma house ruler it would be benefic, but its own nature as a planet might not always be harmonious. In such a case, the Sun at times might become problematic, however it would still be auspicious, overall.

After dharma come the artha houses. Artha represents practical resources which support us, and its element is earth. Taurus, the 2nd sign of the zodiac, is a durable earthy sign which considers stability essential, and whose keywords are sustaining energy. The 2nd house shows things that give us stability, like family, the confidence and happiness developed in childhood, and resources like financial assets. This suggests the 2nd house shows support that we receive thanks to the love and support we have given other people in the past, just like we are normally born in a good family as a consequence of our good actions. The 2nd house is also that of speech – the power of words and communication to sustain something. On a more subtle level, the 2nd represents mental resources, like steadfastness and loyalty.

The other artha houses, the 6th and 10th, relate to Virgo and Capricorn in the natural zodiac. Like the 2nd, they are practical houses: artha is especially connected to karma yoga. Yogananda said "Every action, every thought, reaps its own corresponding reward." Every action and thought can become karma yoga, guided from within, with no selfish desire or attachment to receive its fruits. I mentioned that my Jupiter in Capricorn sometimes expresses its expansiveness on a practical level, by cooking for friends. Capricorn is my 6th house, whose influence and sensitivity to earthy physical things is like Virgo's; both sign and house have the capacity to express a subtle energy through a physical medium (like food).

We have seen earlier that the 6th house relates to practical techniques, obstacles, and service. If we have strong dharma houses, we might have great opportunities spontaneously offered to us, a consequence of good karma we have created in the past. Instead, if we have a strong 6th house we'll probably encounter many obstacles, but we will be strong and successful in overcoming them. Although both the 6th and 10th houses relate to work, the 6th is closer in meaning to humble and serviceful work, not necessarily recognized in a public way. The 10th is a public, visible house, so it indicates status as well as work and career. Of course the 10th can also be serviceful, but it will probably be more visible as it is energetically stronger.

Artha houses are followed by kama houses. Kama is desire, attraction, motivation, which can be more or less spiritualized. Its element is air, the same of the heart chakra, which is the seat of chitta. The heart chakra is where our feelings and our likes and dislikes are centered. The first kama house, the 3rd, is that of personal motivation, directed energy, courage, and communication; it is also the house of siblings and friends. Siblings can lead to some loss of attention from mother, and the 3rd house is the 12th house (loss) from the 4th (mother); they also are an opportunity to be unselfish, another 12th house meaning.

The 3rd house is similar to Gemini, the mutable air sign of Mercury, which is interested, motivated and sociable. A strong Gemini gives an inclination to develop a subtle and flexible intellect. Swami Kriyananda has Gemini ascendant and he has written and talked about yoga and other innumerable topics with extreme clarity and wisdom. The 3rd house is also the house of communication through writing, in fact he has Moon in the 3rd house, in Leo. The Moon is an important planet and Leo is a good placement for it; in Leo it is perhaps not as strong as it would be in Taurus or Cancer, by sign, but it is still well placed.

The mutable character of Gemini makes it also sensitive: as Drupada notes, this sign can develop extreme mental restlessness if it doesn't manage the information overload available in our age. As a Mercury sign, it benefits especially from pratyahara, interiorization.

The other kama houses are the 7th (Libra) and 11th (Aquarius). The 7th house, being that of relationships, shows the kind of energy we are attracted to: for example one of my friends has Libra ascendant, and all her recent boyfriends had either Mars or Sun in Aries. The reason we find attractive the sign of the 7th house is that we are instinctively looking for balance, and that sign indicates opposite and complementary qualities to the ascendant, which represents ourself.

The 11th house is the house of groups and communities (it is the 2nd house of family from the 10th house of public life). It also indicates gains as well as the realization of our goals and desires. It is an upachaya house, which means its meanings will improve with time. As the house of kama that relates to broader realities, it can indicate our motivated energy expressed unselfishly, for the benefit of all. From the karmic rewards of such good actions we receive the gains associated with a strong 11th house.

The 11th house has a natural link to Aquarius. Aquarius is the fixed air sign of Saturn; it shares with Leo a natural inclination of feeling connected with higher realities, however where Leo's focus is personal, Aquarius' nature is impersonal.

The air element is colored by feelings in the sign of Venus, by intellect in the sign of Mercury, and by impersonal wisdom in the sign of Saturn. Aquarius is naturally related to knowledge and humanitarian concerns, and if strong and positive, sharing of wisdom. For example, *Adelle (on page 94) has the ascendant ruler, Venus, in the 10th house of career in Aquarius, and she has a desire to be a medical doctor. She has some work experience in medical research, and it's possible this would progress into medical school, or she might become interested in energetic healing or spiritual counselling. Swami Sri Yukteswar had Moon and Jupiter in Aquarius, and his wisdom and humanitarian concerns are apparent.

The 11th house is that of communities. Communities are formed intentionally by groups of people who have some ideals in common, but even communities which are not entirely intentional, like a town or country, still share some group karma, or those people wouldn't have been attracted in the same place. This group karma is but a collection of subconscious ideas shared by individuals, thus there's a natural link between Aquarius, a sign concerned with sharing of ideas and wisdom, and the 11th house.

After kama, we have the moksha houses, the fourth and last group. Moksha is liberation, search for happiness and joy; its element is water. The first moksha house, the 4th house (Cancer), is inner happiness and emotional state of being. Generally speaking, if we have a strong 4th house we'll be naturally cheerful and content. A dark cloud might pass by, but our good habit of inner contentment will help us through a rough time.

In the next moksha house, the 8th (Scorpio), the search for happiness becomes more intense: it is the house of transformation, and it can be profound and perceptive. It is also called the house of death, as death is but a transformation, the soul shedding its body to go in the astral realms. If our response to a strong 8th house is spiritual, it will aid us in reaching a deeper intensity in

Chapter Nine

meditation and inner joy. An egoic response can find us looking for joy in the wrong places, with destructive passion. Drupada notes the 8th house has a relational nature, where we seek to become one with our partner. Scorpio is more comfortable with a few close friends than with many, more superficial social interactions.

The 8th house is not energetically strong, as it is a house of transformation. However, it is a house where we become involved, for good or for bad, so it can be especially difficult if taken in the wrong direction. Although not innately strong, the 8th, like any other house, can become strong if its sign and ruler are strong.

The last moksha house is the 12th (Pisces), and it is a house of spirituality and liberation; it also indicates foreign countries, as when we travel abroad we can lose some of our egoic identity. For example, Adelle (on page 94) has the 4th house ruler, Sun, exalted in the 12th house. Her 4th house of inner happiness has a direct connection to the spiritual 12th house, so she was drawn to spirituality at a relatively young age. The strength of her 12th house is also indicated by the fact that she eventually went on to live in a different country to that where she spent her childhood.

The 12th house is also a house of hidden things and seclusion, it is a private house, not public; the 4th and 8th share this same trait in their own way. The 4th house is comfortable at home; the 8th can be secret because it seeks intensity of experience, which can be diluted by becoming public; the 12th house downright shuns the limelight. This is not to say that people with several planets in the 12th house cannot become publicly known, but if they do, they will likely be reluctant at first. If they are spiritually advanced, they will eventually accept their public visibility as a way to transcend their ego and be humble channels of expression. It's difficult for those with a strong 12th house to fall into boastful pride, like Leo might; instead they will probably have to boost their low confidence, a problem that a strong Leo normally doesn't have.

The 12th is the house of loss: if we respond to its energy in a negative way, we'll seek to lose ourselves into worldly experiences; if our response is positive we'll lose ourselves in expansive joy in God.

Chapter Ten

Houses and elements

We have seen how each of the house kinds, dharma, artha, kama and moksha, has an affinity with one of the four elements. Assigning an element to each house is not just a theoretical exercise. The elements weave a real connection between houses, signs, planets and chakras.

Kama, our desires, expands evermore like air; air is also the element of the heart chakra, which holds onto the things we desire to have, and those we desire to avoid. Air moves in the wind and drives change, creating storms and moving clouds and pollen, yet its fundamental nature remains the same, much like desires. Our desires change throughout a lifetime, or even just a day, but their nature is always constant, an illusory promise of happiness. The air chakra is that of Venus, and the position of Venus in a chart shows something that we especially love and desire.

For example, in my chart Venus is in Taurus, my 10th house. This shows a desire for stability, as Taurus is fixed earth: I've always had a wish to settle down in a nice cosy home with a garden, growing flowers and vegetables. The 10th house is status and career, and my ego has often desired recognition. Egoistic recognition is based on the delusion that relative status matters, but in reality it does not necessarily bring any happiness. That desire could also involve the wish to do a good job in a position of responsibility, but attachment to material accomplishments does not bring happiness or wisdom, either.

Saturn indicates attachments and it is with Venus in my chart, which shows the desire for recognition was excessively strong, and it would not have been beneficial for me to have it realized as it would have strengthened my ego. My response to the teachings of Saturn has caused the meanings of the 10th house, career, status,

Chapter Ten

and even just having a job, to be blocked or delayed time after time. This lesson is for me to understand that recognition is a desire of the ego. In the Bhagavad Gita, the sacred text of India, it is said God is pleased even by the gift of a leaf, if offered with love and devotion – there is no need for grandiosity.

Swami Kriyananda notes how Taurus is driven by a desire to fix things around it to find security, until it realizes real security lies in the soul. My happiness deepened when I started letting go of my attachment to the 10th house.

Kama is also motivation: air signs are driven by their search for knowledge or ideals. Gemini is curious, Libra wants to realize its ideal of inner harmony, and Aquarius seeks to acquire and share knowledge.

Similar reflections can be made for artha, dharma and moksha. For example, moksha is the search for happiness, and happiness is not something we can define rationally, but rather a way we feel. The nature of moksha is then closer to water than to other elements, and water signs are instinctively aware of its importance.

Although it is more useful, in general, to categorize the houses by their kind, it is interesting to briefly look how the houses interact with the signs only from the point of view of the elements.

The houses and signs each have their own element, which can coincide, or not. Dharma is fire, artha is earth, kama is air, moksha is water. The 1st house is a dharma house, so its element is always fire. If the ascendant is in a fire sign (Aries, Leo or Sagittarius), the 1st house will be of the same element of its sign. This only happens for fire ascendants.

For Aries ascendants, the 4th house, a moksha (water) house, is in Cancer, a water sign. For Leo ascendants, the 4th will be in Scorpio, also a water sign. All the moksha houses of fire ascendants fall into water signs, all the artha houses fall into earth signs, and all the kama houses in air signs. For any other ascendant, the element of the houses and of their signs doesn't coincide. For earth ascendants, the 4th house always falls in a fire sign. In fact, earth ascendants have all the moksha houses in fire signs. There are a few insights to be gained from this.

Fire ascendants are not known for their innate tact, and their search for inner happiness (moksha) involves connecting to their feelings and intuition, as well as the more gentle and compassionate energy of water. All their moksha (water) houses fall into water signs.

Fire ascendants desire knowledge: their kama houses are in air signs. Air can be detached, which can help fire ascendants in their search for wisdom, but air can also be aloof and hinder them in making a deeper connection with water. A lot depends on our response to the energy of the elements.

For water ascendants the houses of moksha fall into air signs. Their search for happiness involves developing the right balance between feelings and intellect, and acquiring the wisdom of detachment from excessive emotions.

For earth ascendants the moksha houses are in fire signs: their search for happiness involves developing their drive, willpower and energy. The fact that their 12th house, the moksha house of liberation, is in a fire sign, suggests they ultimately have to transcend any attachment to form, much like burning it in fire. However, this is true for all of us, we all have to transcend attachment to form. While these and other similar considerations about the elements can help us gain a working knowledge of astrology, we should not use them as fixed concepts of prominent importance. The zodiac is full of subtle connections. To search them all is perhaps to lose sight of the fact that they are important only as an aid in our search for God.

Somebody with Aries ascendant could have strong water qualities and be most kind, maybe indicated by Jupiter exalted in Cancer in the 4th house; or they might not have any planet in water signs and be kind persons because of their innate spirituality, or determined efforts to be so.

The reason I mentioned these general notes about the elements of the houses is that fire, earth, air and water form an elemental basis of the concepts of dharma, artha, kama and moksha. It is useful to understand the qualities of fire when learning about dharma, and vice versa, so that we can form an intuitive connection between them in our mind. However, when actually reading a chart I find it more useful to think about houses in terms of dharma, artha,

Chapter Ten

kama and moksha, and to use the elements only for the signs.

Every chart should be read with new intuition, without trying to force onto it any previous concept we have acquired. These concepts merely form the basis of a language through which our intuition can guide us in understanding the specific energy of each chart.

Chapter Eleven

Planets and deities

In a poem to his guru, Yogananda writes: "If all the gods are displeased, yet thou art pleased, I am safe in the fortress of thy pleasure. And if all the gods protect me behind the parapets of their blessings, yet I receive not thy benedictions, I am an orphan left to pine spiritually in the ruins of thy displeasure."

Yogananda always makes it clear that devotion to God is the most important thing. Sometimes we fall into the mistake of believing that things other than God can give us security, and this is true also for astrology. It is practical to study the stars and their influence, however we should not forget that our devotion to God is more powerful than any star.

The physical stars and planets have no consciousness of themselves, however they have a more subtle counterpart that does have consciousness, so in a way they are living beings, just like our body has no consciousness but is alive thanks to our soul. Yogananda said the planets are in the charge of divine astral beings, manifestations of different aspects of God. This may seem strange, as in this age we are brought up to think that anything which does not exist in a human body is devoid of consciousness. Even souls who are currently not in physical bodies are tucked away in some abstract, far away place, up there with the stars, which we call astral world – that's the etymology of astral, from astrum, star.

Yet consciousness is everywhere, it exists independently of a body, so it shouldn't be too surprising that some of the most advanced astral beings work in creation as angels, carrying out tasks necessary to maintain the universe. These, also, are some of the gods Yogananda mentions. They are described as deities in many stories which shed further light on signs and planets.

One such story describes the birth of Mercury from Soma (the Moon), and Tara, the wife of Brihaspati, (Jupiter). This seemingly illicit affair should be seen through the lens of myth interpretation, as deities only represent different aspects of consciousness, not human beings. Brihaspati is the priest of the gods, busy performing religious ceremonies. Tara is the personification of Brihaspati's feelings, she is the sensitive, feminine side of Jupiter.

Tara is unsatisfied with what seems to be dry renunciation of the world, and is attracted to Soma, which represents enjoyment, whether of creation or of the divine nectar of spiritual bliss. Thus Mercury is born, and Jupiter, being charmed by its intelligence, adopts it. Mercury is a blend of Jupiter and Moon; its Moon side is normally occupied with the changeable creation, but it also has the potential to develop a deeper spiritual wisdom, through its Jupiter side.

For example, Gemini, Mercury's sign, is naturally inclined to intellectual curiosity, but its vision can be expanded by the upward aspiration to divine wisdom of Sagittarius, its opposite sign, ruled by Jupiter. Conversely, both Jupiter signs benefit from the focused power of discrimination possible in Mercury signs. The enthusiasm of Sagittarius can benefit from the rational intellect of Gemini. If we follow our enthusiasm blindly, we might become inspired to follow a course of action which we later find was ill-advised, and that we could have avoided had we just used some common sense.

Because of the affinity between houses and the natural zodiac, a similar comment can be made between the 3rd house of personal motivation and the 9th house of divine grace. Relying too much on personal effort can make us forget that nothing is possible without divine grace, while waiting lazily for help from above is not going to get us there anytime soon – unless we have a store of good karma from previous efforts in the past.

Another myth finds the wife of the Sun unhappy with the scorching strength of his light. She leaves her own shadow at home

Planets and deities

and departs. The Sun radiates light; as Drupada says, it gives and never takes, but is not known for its sensitivity. When the Sun comes home he doesn't notice the substitution and thus Saturn is born, son of light (the Sun) and of shadow, the material world.

This story shows that Saturn has two sides: light and shadow. The shadow side represents the material plane, in fact Saturn rules the earth chakra at the bottom of the spine. The earthy qualities of Saturn, concentration and focus, are essential on the spiritual path. However, the earthy side has also a negative connotation, contrasted to the other side made of light. Saturn is often the planet that brings difficulties, representing the downward pull of energy toward material form. A negative Saturn is the most difficult planet to respond to, as it draws us down and is rather unmovable – being earthy it doesn't respond quickly to our efforts.

The purpose of most yoga techniques is to uplift our energy, creating an upward pull in the spine which raises our consciousness towards the divine light of the spiritual eye, at the top of the spine. By raising our energy we move closer to the light side of Saturn, which can give us unshakable peace. To do so requires wisdom and understanding, and represents the victory of light over shadow.

Another group of deities directly relevant to astrology have been mentioned by Yogananda, who described how they are related to the chakras.

The earth chakra is that of Ganesha, god of success. Ganesha's figure is chubby and his head is that of an elephant. His temperament is benevolent, wise and protecting of those who ask his help. His brother is Kartikeya (Mars), a powerful warrior protector of the gods. Mars is exalted in Capricorn, in the earth chakra; the planet of courage finds spiritual success in the chakra of Ganesha.

A small story illustrates the difference between Ganesha and Mars. The two brothers were playing with their father, Shiva, when he asked them to circle the universe three times. He hadn't even finished explaining the challenge when Mars had already started running. Ganesha, not able to compete with the physical

Chapter Eleven

prowess of his brother, simply walked three times around Shiva, declaring that his father, as the aspect of God which transcends creation, was the real essence of the universe.

This story shows that Ganesha and Saturn are connected through the earth chakra. Saturn is the planet which brings us obstacles, but it is also a planet of wisdom: Ganesha is invoked for its power to overcome obstacles through wisdom. Ganesha cannot compete with the speed of Mars. Similarly, Saturn is slow: it is the planet farther away from the Sun and takes more than 29 years to complete its orbit. Drupada perceptively says that Saturn's purpose is to slow us down to the present moment, citing Yogananda: "Forget the past for it's gone from your domain, forget the future, it is beyond your reach. Control the present, live supremely well now. It will whitewash away the dark past and compel the future to be bright. This is the way of the wise."

After the earth chakra of Saturn, we have the water chakra of Jupiter; its deity is Shakti, goddess of power. Shakti is Cosmic Nature, Aum, Divine Mother and the infinite power of manifestation. Jupiter is the most generous planet in manifesting spiritual and material prosperity, because it acts as a channel for Shakti. In several stories the gods turn to an aspect of Shakti for help with problems no one else can solve.

Then we have the fire chakra, that of Mars; its deity is Surya-Creator, god of fire. Surya is the Sun, which is exalted in Aries, a sign of the fire chakra. The fiery Sun is the light at the point between the eyebrows, where we concentrate to uplift our energy. The Sun is willpower and creative energy, it is strong in both Leo and Aries. However Leo, sign of the spiritual eye, is fixed, while Aries is active. In Leo the Sun is happy just to shine, while in Aries it wants to be active and express its creativity. The active fire of Sun in Aries is like Brahma, the Creator.

It follows that in Libra, the sign opposite, the Sun is debilitated. Libra is in the heart chakra, which is a receptive chakra. The Sun radiates, it is not receptive: in Libra the Sun can be indecisive and not confident. However, Sun in Libra is an opportunity to deepen our concern for others, and to learn to act with inner balance and well thought-out purpose.

Planets and deities

The next chakra is the air chakra, of Venus; its deity is Vishnu. Venus is joy, happiness, beauty; it is naturally associated with benevolent goddesses such as Lakshmi, goddess of prosperity and consort of Vishnu, who preserves and sustains creation. Bhagavan Krishna, an incarnation of Vishnu, had Moon in Taurus, and he was irresistibly beautiful and charming. The Moon, in fact, is exalted in Taurus, sign of the heart chakra; in its sign of exaltation it is happy, joyful and charming.

Venus, instead, is exalted in Pisces, sign of the water chakra. Our heart, joy and sense of beauty are expanded in Pisces, sign of universal compassion and empathy. Incidentally, Krishna, whose ascendant was also in Taurus, a Venus sign, is often depicted as playing the flute; this is the astral sound of the water chakra (Pisces) which can be heard at times in meditation.

Venus is debilitated in the sign opposite Pisces, Virgo: excessive attention to rationality can suffocate our joy and feelings. We should remember not to respond to Venus in Virgo by encouraging in us a habit of worrying and critical judging. We should rather soften any such tendency with trust and surrender to the compassion and love of God, so that we, too, can manifest such qualities. Venus in Virgo then represents discrimination in controlling our heart desires, our likes and dislikes.

In contrast to Jupiter, who is described in stories as the spiritual teacher of the gods, Venus is the teacher of those who do not always follow dharma, as they are still enmeshed in the delusion of creation. They follow their desires, but they, too, might be receptive to spiritual advice, especially from Venus, which is sweet, charming and attractive. In one story, Venus is able, with great effort, to realize a strong desire of its daughter, but she still does not find happiness. This illustrates how Venus, a benevolent planet, might realize some of our desires, but real happiness can still elude us, because the only real lasting happiness is spiritual inner happiness.

The last deity Yogananda identifies is Shiva, the dissolver of creation, for the ether chakra. The ether chakra is that of Mercury, in fact both its signs, Gemini and Virgo, are mutable (Shiva) signs. Ether is the most subtle of the five elements, and mutable

Chapter Eleven

signs have the most subtle modality. Shiva is often described as a renunciate yogi, and when we achieve pratyahara we, too, withdraw from creation.

All the different deities we encountered in these stories are aspects of God, taking different names to express different states of consciousness. Their qualities are meant to remind us of our real identity as souls, rising above the influence of any star.

Yogananda several times started a new endeavour when the stars were unfavorable, to prove how the spiritual powers of the soul are always stronger. Every time he succeeded. He did state, however, that a stronger effort might be needed when the stars are unfavorable rather than favorable.

A beautiful example of how devotion can defeat any obstacle is Hanuman. Hanuman's body is that of a monkey, symbolizing our restless mind. However, he is always in perfect control of his mind, his every thought and action following dharma. He is completely devoted to serving Rama, an incarnation of Vishnu. In the ancient story narrated in the Ramayana, Rama's wife is abducted and Hanuman completes astonishing features of strength and cunning in helping with the rescue. He symbolizes the perfection we can achieve with complete devotion to God.

Hanuman is the son of Vayu, the god of air. Air is prana, life force, and Hanuman possesses such incredible strength precisely because of his perfect control of prana – pranayama. As a child, he jumped all the way to the Sun; as an adult, he could lift mountains. He was also an unparalleled diplomat and devotional singer. For all this, he was most humble.

The saint Valmiki had written the story of the life of Rama. Having learnt that Hanuman had written his own version of the Ramayana, the saint asked to read it and was saddened at realizing it was of a much greater quality than his own. Without hesitation, Hanuman threw his own version into the sea.

Hanuman's devotion is so great that his mind and heart have no space for anything other than Rama. He never has fear of anything;

Planets and deities

not even Saturn can affect him. In one story, the personification of a negative and malefic Saturn tries to cause suffering to Hanuman. The monkey god defeats him without effort, letting him go only after Saturn promises to not afflict anybody who invokes Hanuman, the embodiment of devotion and selfless service to God.

Chapter Twelve

Rahu and Ketu

A chart is made of all signs, and balancing each of the six pairs of opposites is always important, whether or not they are occupied by planets. For example, in my chart (on page 79) Virgo and Pisces are empty. However, my Mercury's signs are stronger than those of Jupiter, because Mercury, which shares the strength of an exalted Sun, is stronger than Jupiter, which is debilitated in the 6th house. This means that my chart is more inclined toward the rational analysis of Virgo, rather than toward the all-encompassing universal feelings of Pisces. Reading my chart made me more aware of the need to balance rationality with compassion.

Signs which are occupied by planets, however, deserve special attention. My Aries, with its exalted Sun, is stronger than my Libra. As a consequence I make an effort (not always successful) to be kinder and more diplomatic in all circumstances, especially in situations where there is a conflict with other people. Aries is a doer, its attitude is "do it first, think about it later, if at all", Libra is also a doer, but of a different kind, its attitude is rather "think about it first, and then do it." If my Aries and Libra are unbalanced, they usually sway on the side of excessive Aries: I tend to be more comfortable doing something, instead of reflecting on what it is that I should be doing.

When considering opposite signs, we can get an idea of which of the two is more influential by looking at which of their rulers is stronger. In my chart, Venus is in its own sign in the 10th house, while Mars is in the 7th house, neither in its own sign nor exalted. Taking only this into account Venus would be stronger. However, Venus is in the very first degree, just entering the sign, and it is with Saturn, a planet that can be constrictive. Saturn can constrict the Sun's light, so it is not too positive for Leo ascendants, increasing the likelihood that its influence will be obstructive; it is also rather strong by being in the 10th house. Overall, in this chart Saturn is overshadowing Venus. As a consequence, Mars and Venus are roughly of similar strength, though Mars is slightly more influential because it is opposite the ascendant. In any case, Aries is surely stronger than Libra because of Sun's exaltation.

Learning to understand which sign is stronger can be useful when interpreting Rahu and Ketu. The pair of opposite signs which they occupy is important for everybody to balance. Rahu and Ketu are always opposite each other and they have opposite effects on our consciousness. Rahu draws our energy up and out, Ketu down and in. In yoga we want to maintain a strong uplifting flow in our energetic spine, avoiding a strong downward flow toward materialism and ego-consciousness. However, it is also natural for our energy to regularly flow up and down: each time we inhale, energy flows up, and when we exhale, energy flows down. What matters is the intention behind this flow of energy.

An upward flow is cheerful and life-affirming, however, if it is directed out of ourselves, then it is involved with the world; the question then becomes whether this involvement is selfless, or selfish.

The upward and outward flow of energy of Rahu involves us in the world, either toward selfish sense enjoyment, ambition and material desires, or toward selfless caring for the world and service to God.

With the downward and inward flow of Ketu we withdraw from the world, either in selfish rejection, life-negation and depressive separation from everything, or as meditative interiorization, withdrawal from over-involvement in the world, and reception of higher insights descending into our consciousness from above.

When Rahu and Ketu are out of balance, we alternate between the two sides, not entirely of our own free will. If Rahu's sign is stronger and we keep focusing on it, but devote no time to Ketu, we'll be forced into a situation where we have to engage with Ketu. This might manifest as actual physical circumstances, or as a strong inner compulsion. For example, if we party all the time and do not find solitude appealing, something might happen which forces us to have some quiet time on our own. The same is valid if Ketu is stronger: you likely prefer to be on your own, perhaps reading a book, but you might feel lonely and have a strong desire to go to that party, even though you know you won't feel too comfortable there.

Rahu and Ketu, when out of balance, have this compulsive nature, to force us into situations that seek to rebalance their opposite signs. Rahu and Ketu are not physical planets, so they are more likely to influence us through our mind rather than external circumstances, however that is not always true.

Usually, if there is a big imbalance it is quite obvious in a chart. For example, I have Ketu with Moon in Gemini, which puts Rahu in Sagittarius (page 79). The Moon, our mind, is an important point, second only to the ascendant. Because of its importance, having Rahu or Ketu with the Moon makes them very influential. In fact, for a great part of my life I have had a strong Ketu nature. I was extremely introverted, and I felt separated from everything and everyone. Conversely, when I started meditating it was relatively easy for me to establish a steady habit of daily meditations. Time and the practice of yoga change things, and I am not as introverted anymore, though I'm still more comfortable with smaller, rather than bigger, groups of people.

Ketu is the planet of insight without words, its symbol is a yogi meditating with no head; it can give strong powers of perception. When Ketu is with the Moon, this is not always easy. I would sense too much from people, and I could not put it into words, not even to myself; it was often uncomfortable. Only when I developed a strong meditation practice I started to feel more at ease. If we have troubles with Ketu, it is helpful to remember that devotion makes our aura strong, which is the best protection.

Those with a strong Rahu are usually extroverted and comfortable in social situations, but they should be careful not to lose themselves in outward commitments, as excessive world involvement makes us restless and eventually unhappy. A yogi wants to be in the world, but not of the world; part of it, but not possessed by it. Yogananda said: "Mental restlessness results from an outward focus of awareness. Restlessness itself guarantees that happiness will remain elusive."

When we make an effort to balance Rahu and Ketu they start functioning together. As Drupada said, Ketu is then insight we receive from God, and Rahu is sharing our blessing with the world. A balanced and positive Ketu is associated with meditation and moksha (liberation), and a balanced Rahu with selfless service. We should keep in mind this teaching of Yogananda: too much service makes us restless and too much meditation makes us selfish.

The different direction of flow of the energy of Rahu and Ketu also indicates a subtle difference between the two. When we are too much on the side of Ketu we are drawn too much downward and inside; at first it will feel comfortable and familiar, but soon we will feel isolated, lonely and stagnating. A conscious effort to develop our Rahu side will be liberating, we will see it as a new interesting experience.

If we are too much on the side of Rahu we will be drawn outward and upward. Without the balancing effect of a positive Ketu, Rahu will make us scattered, always looking for something outside ourselves. If supported by Ketu, though, even those with a strong Rahu will find that Rahu's sign is their direction of growth, because it takes us away from what's familiar. We don't need to abandon everything that is familiar and comfortable, but some of what is familiar is not actually beneficial. A bird might consider its cage familiar.

The common condition for human beings is to be identified to a greater or lesser degree with our ego. Dissolving our ego is, for the ego, an uncomfortable process of leaving something familiar for the unknown; that is why Rahu, taking us away from excessive familiarity, indicates a house and sign of spiritual growth. If we accept this process then it does not feel compulsive and uncomfortable anymore, but rather liberating and inspiring.

Chapter Twelve

For example, I've always had an inclination toward Gemini. Although Gemini is a sociable sign that likes communication, I have Ketu in it, which is not a social planet, meaning I was concentrated on other sides of Gemini. I was comfortable spending hours reading books in which the author created a smart and believable world. I liked watching movies and TV shows, and most of all playing computer games. Due to their interactive nature, games can be very immersive. I recall one game, *Prince of Persia* (2008), set in a large oasis in the desert. During the course of the story I ended up in a spire, amongst the tallest towers in a royal palace. The view was immense and breathtaking. The night was clear and the stars and moon gently lit the soft sand dunes, extending endlessly in the desert; a wide river was flowing behind the majestic palace, falling toward a high waterfall out of sight. The top floor of the spire was open on all sides, giving an encompassing view of the soothing palpable expanding moon, the gravity-defying fairy tale architecture, and the green oasis by the waterside. Calmness and beauty were so pervasive that they inspired me in several meditations. These are Ketu perceptions without words.

My higher education in physics was also, clearly, a Gemini activity. However, as in all things done in excess, too much Gemini was feeling increasingly stagnating. I made a conscious effort to develop my Sagittarius, to be more enthusiastic and uplifted, and I started feeling happier. This doesn't mean I stopped using my intellect, but rather that I would not overuse it. Sometimes I would get a bad feeling about doing something, but still go through with it because it seemed the rational thing to do. Now I follow my intuition when I have a strong uplifting feeling, but I also test its accuracy with my intellect. I try to have a more universal and expansive view of things, and be happy just because, with no particular reason. These are always good things to keep in mind, however, if I had Ketu in Sagittarius, I would focus instead on whether my enthusiasm is directed in a fruitful way. It would be useful, in that case, to make a special effort to develop the critical insight of Gemini; with Ketu in Sagittarius, enthusiasm would probably come more naturally to me than rationality.

As another example lets look at Adelle's chart (on page 94). Ketu is in Virgo; Rahu, Jupiter and Mercury are in Pisces. Jupiter is strong in own sign, while Mercury is debilitated in Pisces. Mercury receives some strength from Jupiter, so it is not as weak as if it were alone in Pisces, however, overall, Pisces is clearly stronger than Virgo. Rahu's side is then stronger, in fact Adelle is sociable and extroverted. Depending on the moment, she's capable of following her feelings and intuition (Pisces) but also deliberate with careful analysis (Virgo). Overall Pisces is more evident in her personality, but she has some Virgo moments as well. She's practicing yoga and meditation, so she is learning to balance the two sides.

The fact that Mercury and Jupiter are together indicates that the integration of Rahu and Ketu is likely not to be as challenging as in my chart, where Mercury is in a sign of Mars and Jupiter in a sign of Saturn – my Mercury and Jupiter are not in direct communication.

In any case, her Rahu's side is stronger, so she feels closer to Pisces than Virgo. The compassion and devotion of Pisces is also where she feels more spiritual growth – Rahu is always the direction of growth even when it is stronger than Ketu.

The balance between Rahu and Ketu is affected by any planet in their sign, as well as the rulers of those two signs. If neither Rahu nor Ketu are stronger in an obvious way, it does not necessarily mean that they are balanced; they might still be swinging. However, it does mean that it is probably going to be easier to achieve integration of their energies.

Rahu and Ketu act especially on the mind because they are not physical planets, they are intangible. They do correspond, though, to certain astronomical points: the intersections between the paths of the Moon and the Sun in the Earth sky. These are the only points where eclipses can occur: a Sun eclipse during a new Moon, when the Moon is between the Earth and the Sun; or a Moon eclipse during a full Moon, when the Earth is between the Moon and the Sun.

Because the chart is seen from the point of view of the Earth, the Sun and Moon are in the same sign for the new Moon and in opposite signs for the full Moon; when this happens close to Rahu and Ketu an eclipse can occur. For example, around the 20th of May of this year, 2012, there was a Sun eclipse: Sun, Moon and Ketu were in Taurus.

Eclipses are special occurrences where Rahu and Ketu become stronger and can make us too open to outside influences. Everybody's energy can also become very much withdrawn inward, as either the light of the Sun or that of the Moon is hidden. Thus it is better not to travel, or be too involved with outward activities during eclipses, if at all possible; although, they are a good time for meditation.

Because of their association with eclipses, Rahu and Ketu are called shadow planets. They are also called lunar nodes because of their astronomical meaning. Looking at the solar system from the outside, the plane of the orbit of the Earth around the Sun is called the ecliptic plane. The plane of the orbit of the Moon around the Sun is inclined about 5 degrees to the ecliptic plane. This means that the Moon's orbit is half above and half below the ecliptic plane, and crosses it at two points, opposite each other. The point where the Moon moves from below the ecliptic to above, is called ascending or north lunar node – this is Rahu. The point opposite, where the Moon descends below the ecliptic, is called descending or south node – this is Ketu.

Rahu and Ketu are always opposite, and their motion is retrograde in the chart, backward compared to the other planets. This influences their characteristics: they are a bit different from normal, so any planet together with either of them could acquire some original or unusual trait.

Rahu and Ketu

When other planets are retrograde they, too, change their energy: it is more inwardly directed. A retrograde planet tends towards introspection. For example, retrograde Mercury can give an introspective intellect. This means that the energy of retrograde planets is not as strong in the outward direction. A retrograde Jupiter is more inclined to give prosperity of the mind rather than material prosperity. A retrograde Saturn might mean that our karmic lessons are less on the material plane and more in our thoughts.

All physical planets in the solar system always rotate in the same direction, however from the point of view of the Earth they sometimes appear to retrace their steps. This can happen to Mercury, Venus, Mars, Jupiter and Saturn. When they appear to move backwards in the sky they are retrograde. In the South Indian notation, planets move clockwise, and counterclockwise when retrograde. Retrograde planets are closer to Earth, astronomically, so they can be a bit stronger than when in direct motion.

Another name for Rahu and Ketu comes from the story of their origin. The gods were busy looking for the nectar of immortality and enlisted the help of a snake-like dragon who also wanted it. When the nectar was found the gods cut the dragon in half, but the dragon had already drunk some nectar so it was immortal. The head of the dragon became Rahu, and the body and tail Ketu. This illustrates why Ketu is not eloquent with words, while Rahu can be too airy, "in the head", ambitious and restless. However, Rahu can also inspire us to achieve something good. This story makes obvious the need to unite the Dragon's Head and Tail, that is, to balance Rahu and Ketu.

A good house placement for the nodes is Rahu in the 6th and Ketu in the 12th, the house of practical service and the house of liberation. For the same reason, Rahu in Virgo and Ketu in Pisces are also good. A very strong position by sign is Rahu in Gemini and Ketu in Sagittarius, as Rahu is airy in character and Gemini can be subtle in understanding, while the uplifting fiery energy of Sagittarius agrees with Ketu's spiritual aspirations. However, Drupada notes that one must be able to harness the subtlety of this placement, otherwise the mutable character of Gemini can enhance the tendency of Rahu to be restless.

Another good position is Rahu in Taurus and Ketu in Scorpio. Both Ketu and Scorpio are attracted to depth of consciousness in an experiential rather than intellectual way, while Taurus' stability can calm Rahu and be a good channel to express its energy.

Rahu is also comfortable in Aquarius, as it is an air sign interested in acquiring and sharing knowledge. Rahu likes to be involved in the world, so it is happy in the 10th house; it also likes the 11th house for it is a kama goal-oriented house (Rahu is driven).

Ketu, for his search of spiritual knowledge, has an affinity with Ganesha, while Rahu with Durga. Durga is an aspect of Divine Mother, a powerful warrior goddess who always defeats the demons of ignorance; she is very protective of those who ask for her help with devotion. A negative Rahu represents a dynamic and selfish search for happiness in the material world, which will attract troubles and leave us in need of protection. When we invoke with sincerity the fierce motherly protection of Divine Mother, we are humbly surrendering to Her. Humbleness helps us develop Rahu's positive traits.

Yogananda said: "When a person renounces outward ambitions to seek peace within himself, he may feel a certain fleeting nostalgia for his old, familiar habits. Accustomed as he was formerly to outward busy-ness, simplicity may strike him at times, in the beginning, as stark and unattractive."

Just like Ketu people may be uncomfortable with Rahu outward busy-ness, Rahu people may find Ketu activities unattractive. However, perseverance and balance will bring true happiness.

Chapter Thirteen

Kashiraja's chart

Fire is energy and willpower, which are essential to everybody. However, if we rely too much on our own will we will feel life is a constant struggle. It is true that world delusion is strong and that we have to fight it to find happiness, but we will not get out of it just by trying very hard. The projection of will and energy, by its very nature, is not receptive, but an attitude of receptivity is necessary to receive guidance. Kriyananda said: "The *sensitivity* with which one 'tries just once more', rather than the mere act of repetition, is the real key to success."

Energy and willpower need to be directed and controlled by wisdom, yet if our expression of fire qualities is immature, control is the last thing we want. We consider it an unnecessary constraint, a way to put down our innate exuberance. While it is true that sometimes people unfairly resent our fiery enthusiasm, it is for our own benefit that we should learn wise restraint. Wisdom is not a controlling attitude of curtailing all and every expression of energy and will, but the discrimination of knowing when action is needed and when it would be harmful. Wisdom also guides willpower so that it is not used blindly to pursue endless desires.

In the words of Yogananda: "Self-control at first produces unhappiness because of the separation from the pleasure-yielding senses. After self-control ripens, however, the soul begins to experience finer, happier perceptions and to enjoy itself far more than when it lived identified with the sense-pleasures."

Without control, desires tend to multiply and become increasingly difficult to fulfill, making us frustrated and, eventually, prone to anger. The fire element, more than any other element, can be channeled into habits of anger and impatience. To avoid yielding to such unhealthy emotions, self-control is needed. We should

Chapter Thirteen

keep this in mind, especially if we have strong fire in our chart.

On the other hand, if we have difficulty in expressing willpower we should by all means make every effort to develop it – shying away from life's obstacles will not help us find happiness.

There is a slight difference in the way the two fiery planets, Mars and Sun, relate to self-control, and it depends on their relationship with Saturn, which is the planet of yama, control. Saturn is impersonal, while the most personal planets are Moon and Sun. The Moon, ruling a water sign and representing our feelings, is more receptive than the Sun, which is willful. The Moon's challenge, and key to our happiness, is to achieve the emotional detachment that Saturn symbolizes. The same is true for the Sun, but the focus is more on achieving impersonal self-control of willpower.

Mars and Sun are both fiery, so we can imagine they'll both have some reservations about practising self-control. However, Mars is exalted in Capricorn, sign of Saturn, it is a warrior who relishes a challenge. When Mars realizes that self-control is just another challenge, it is perfectly capable of becoming disciplined. Sun is of course also capable, but, compared to Mars, it can be more resentful of Saturn, as it will perceive any suggestion to exercise control as an unjustified demand.

The Sun has a strong sense of personal authority, while Mars is more self-oblivious, absorbed in its own activities. Mars is independent, but it doesn't consider itself royalty like the Sun does.

Saturn is the most difficult planet for the Sun. I should know because my ascendant is Leo and my Sun is exalted in Aries, so I have an innate fiery nature. But I also have a strong Saturn, in the 10th house of career. Sun and Saturn in this configuration, if they are not getting along, will cause great frustration. If Saturn is blocking the 10th house, the Sun wants to overcome the obstacle by pure application of energy and willpower. But no matter how hard you try, you cannot force people to give you a job. Even a strong Sun can lose its will, and a downcast energy will increase the negativity of Saturn. My efforts became much more fruitful when I finally started to understand that they should be applied to changing myself, not others.

Kashiraja's chart

	Me Su	Ve Sa	Mo Ke
Ma			
Ju			
Ra			

Kashiraja's chart. Leo ascendant is strong because of Sun exalted in Aries, in the 9th house of grace and spirituality. The 9th ruler, Mars, sends its benefic influence on the ascendant. Being Mars, although benefic, it nevertheless needs to practice self-control.

But more than effort is needed. In the words of Yogananda: "By keeping your concentration at the spiritual eye, at the point between the eyebrows, it's possible to develop great will power. But this practice must be combined with, and supported by, the heart's devotion."

The spiritual eye is Leo, the heart is Venus, Taurus and Libra. In my chart Venus is in Taurus, which gives it strength, although it is in the very first degree, so it is sometimes tentative in its strength. Saturn is contractive, and it can constrict Venus with worries. Saturn is a perfectionist, it can make us doubt ourselves, which will exacerbate the tendency to inner insecurity of Taurus, an intrinsic characteristics of that sign. However, if I keep my heart open, then Saturn gives me peace, and any disharmony with the Sun is gone – for a time.

As Yogananda said: "Worries are hard to eliminate. You kill off some and others seem to swarm in seemingly from nowhere." With Saturn it is not enough to learn the lesson once, we have to apply it at every occasion, until there's a permanent change in our consciousness – that is when we have really learnt it. Yogananda continues: "Worries are stupified by calmness and slight happiness, but are completely eradicated by the constant culture of steadfast peace." A positive Saturn gives peace: it is the planet of obstacles, but also of overcoming obstacles.

Saturn, like any other planet, is positive when our energy flows upward, and negative when it flows downward. Sometimes our energy will be flowing up, but something happens which ruins our cheerful mood. Challenges are part of life. When an outward circumstance is obstructing us, be it an adverse astrological influence or another practical obstacle, we can respond to it in an uplifting or downcasting way. Astrology is the study of our response to such difficulties, not as a purely intellectual exercise, but rather as a means to increase our happiness. It is not practical to ignore outward circumstances, and we should do our best to improve them, but our happiness depends above all on the inner attitude with which we confront them.

With a positive response, Venus with Saturn in Taurus can give discrimination in following the heart's desires, as well as great practical skills, because Saturn is methodical and Taurus is earthy and stable.

In other words, Venus can represent desires, and in the fixed earth sign of Taurus it can represent enjoyment of material desires. There's nothing wrong in eating an ice-cream, but desires have a tendency to multiply, and then we rather want three ice-creams. That is when Saturn shows up to bring discipline. We have a choice to control our desires, but we can also just get frustrated at Saturn and refuse to learn to behave. Then we might lose our wallet, or find the ice-cream shop has closed down. Again we have a choice to remain happy and unaffected, or we can complain and become even more unhappy. In one case, Venus and Saturn give discrimination in controlling desires, inner peace and happiness. In the other case, Saturn casts a gloomy shadow on our heart and blocks our energy by excessive contraction. The choice is ours.

Since we are all familiar with our own lives, we can relate the planets in our chart with our own experiences. When looking at a chart of someone we don't know well, a useful way to verify our intuition is to check if there are several indications in the chart which support the same conclusion.

In my chart, it is quite clear that the fire element is strong but the water element, which can balance fire with receptivity, is not as strong. I have no planets in any of the three water signs, and the Moon, a watery receptive planet, is not strong. The strongest of the three water sign rulers is Mars, but it is not a receptive planet and it is in an air sign.

Willpower needs to be balanced by devotion and an open heart, which are especially indicated by Pisces, the sign that gives universal empathy and compassion. In my chart, Jupiter is debilitated in the 6th house, so Pisces is not strong. Overall, this reinforces our initial interpretation of the need to balance the fire of Sun and Mars.

Back to the difficult influence of Saturn, another indication that this planet's influence is excessive is that I have Rahu in a Jupiter sign, Sagittarius. This shows that I will especially benefit by increasing my expression of Jupiter's energy. Jupiter, in a way, is opposite and complementary to Saturn. One of the defining traits of a positive Sagittarius is uplifting enthusiasm and joy. Happiness is what's needed to dissolve the worries of a negative Saturn. The key is to break the feedback loop which makes us respond to a negative Saturn in a negative way, in turn creating even more obstacles.

A positive feedback is the uplifting decision to be happy in every moment, which will dissolve our worries and help us respond to Saturn's energy in a positive way. This positive response will greatly reduce any suffering brought by Saturn, and eventually we will become friends with this profound planet.

A strong, willful Sun may have an attitude of egoistic self-reliance, but human will, no matter how strong, is always limited; it becomes all powerful only when it is attuned with and becomes Divine Will. Attunement is the receptivity of an open heart to be open to divine grace. With effort, will power, and receptivity, we

Chapter Thirteen

will achieve true success. My chart shows an imbalance between receptivity and projection of energy which needs to be corrected.

A related imbalance is between the expansiveness of Jupiter and the contractive powers of Saturn. For Leo ascendants, Jupiter is especially benefic. For each ascendant there are three planets which are especially positive: the rulers of the trine houses, the 1st, 5th and 9th. The ruler of the ascendant signifies self, while the 5th and 9th signs are of the same element of the ascendant, so their rulers are in natural harmony with it. However, we also have to take into consideration the nature of the planets themselves, so if Saturn rules any of these three houses it will be more positive than normal, but it will not lose its status as the strict teacher.

Some might think it is a disadvantage to have a strict planet as one of the benefic trine rulers, for example for Capricorn or Aquarius ascendants. But it can also be an advantage, as the planet which brings us obstacles and lessons is more benefic when ruling a trine, so those obstacles will be easier to overcome. Even then, it's tempting to always blame Saturn, but sometimes it is actually another planet that disrupts Saturn's discipline and concentration.

In any case, for Leo ascendants Saturn can be difficult because it is not naturally friendly with the Sun, and it also rules the 6th house of obstacles. Its specific character as ruler of the 6th house coincides with its intrinsic qualities as a planet. Jupiter's energy is a natural balance for Saturn as it is expansive, and for Leo ascendants it rules the 5th house, a trine.

The necessity to expand our consciousness may seem obvious to a yogi, but I am talking of a subtle and useful difference, the need for balance and moderation. If I had a chart with no strength in fire signs, but a lot of energy in water signs, and especially in Pisces, I would be inclined to be more open, receptive and expansive. A useful focus then would be on having a strong center and developing willpower, so that my expansiveness and receptivity are not too passive or misguided, but remain balanced and open to wholesome influences. However, in my chart the need to strengthen the expansiveness of Sagittarius and Pisces is obvious.

A similar lesson is indicated by Venus with Saturn, where I have to be attentive to not let the contractive energy of Saturn close my heart. If contraction is dominant, then all that is left in my chart is the fire of an unbalanced willpower, as receptivity is expansive in nature and it is reduced by contraction. It may seem that a strong Saturn would be good to discipline the Sun, but without expansion and receptivity, fire is strongly opposed to self-control.

Yet another planet in my chart confirms the need to learn self-control: Mars in Aquarius. It is in the 7th house of relationships, so it can show an occasional argumentative nature – Mars likes to fight. The same can also be indicated by Mercury in Aries: the planet of intellect and communication in a fire sign can be too quick, impulsive and competitive.

However, Mars is positive for Leo ascendants because it rules the 9th house. The intrinsic character of Mars can add too much fire to Leo, but overall the ruler of the 9th house is benefic. The 9th house indicates spirituality, and Aquarius a search for knowledge. Mars in Aquarius, then, is searching for spiritual knowledge. The same is shown by Sun and Mercury in the 9th house: using the light of intellect to attune with Spirit.

When we see repetitions of similar concepts with different planets, we can be confident that it is something noteworthy.

The link between Leo, Aries and Aquarius is a positive loop of energy: the ruler of the ascendant is the Sun, which is in Aries; the ruler of Aries is Mars which is opposite the ascendant. The strength of Mars, Aries and Sun is what has taken me out of the many ruts I fell into, time and again: Aries is the capacity to start anew.

To summarize, in my chart the ascendant is strong because Sun is exalted. If Mars were in a difficult position it would slightly weaken the Sun, but it is in the 7th house, an angular house, so it has some strength. Leo, Aries and Aquarius are fire and air signs, and Mars and Sun are fiery planets, so it is clear that I need to listen and not impose my will. This interpretation is reinforced by the fact that Venus, the planet of the heart chakra, has some strength by being in Taurus and in the 10th house, but can be overshadowed by Saturn. Both the strength of Saturn and that of Sun and Mars can give an attitude of projecting excessive efforts, so I need receptivity and self-control.

In my chart the Sun is in the 9th house with Mercury, and the 9th house ruler is in Aquarius opposite the ascendant. Both the 9th house and Mars indicate a search for knowledge, and a desire to share it with others.

A similar meaning can be valid for Ketu with Moon in Gemini: a positive Ketu is keen on spiritual renunciation and Moon in Gemini has a questioning attitude. My response to Moon with Ketu certainly gave me troubles for a long time, but recurring questioning of everything led me, in the end, to the real happiness of spirituality. Ketu looks for experiential, not intellectual knowledge. It is the *experience* of spirituality that brings happiness.

With a spiritual uplifting mood, Saturn with Venus indicates detachment from desires. A strong Saturn can be balanced by a strong Jupiter, but in my chart Jupiter is debilitated. Drupada said about my Jupiter: "The 6th house, in earthy Capricorn, is similar to Virgo, so it represents the analytical mind. This is where we get questions, as Capricorn can be a little skeptical, but it is also practical. A practical intellect is realistic, but sometimes overanalyzes and gets too caught in the details, losing the Jupiter inspiration."

Jupiter is the planet of niyama. One of the niyamas is cleanliness of mind and not dwelling on anything that may pull the mind down to body consciousness. This is especially important with a strong Saturn because it is the planet at the base of the spine, so if negative, it creates a strong downward flow.

An Indian tradition to improve Saturn is to be especially generous on its day, Saturday. Each planet has an affinity to a certain day, during which its energy is slightly more influential. In order from Monday, the days are ruled by Moon, Mars, Mercury, Jupiter, Venus, Saturn and Sun. The tradition of feeding the poor on Saturday, or really any act of generosity, balances selfish contraction.

The need of focusing on expansiveness and generosity in my chart is also shown by Rahu in Sagittarius. Part of the highest expression of Sagittarius is *living* happiness. In the words of Yogananda: "To seek happiness outside ourselves is like trying to lasso a cloud. Happiness is not a thing: it is a state of mind. It must be lived."

Yogananda had a strong Sagittarian nature. While listening to his talks, you can't help but feel the contagious enthusiasm. Sometimes he would run on stage and ask "how is everybody?" – the answer would be "awake and ready!" In fact he had Leo ascendant, with Sun and Mercury in Sagittarius. You can always feel he is joyful.

There is a slight conflict in my chart because Rahu is stronger in Gemini and Ketu in Sagittarius, and their positions are reversed in my chart. It indicates that initially I had extra difficulty with the nodes. Rahu is the Head of the Dragon, so it is more comfortable than Ketu in a thinking sign like Gemini. Ketu perceives without thought, so it can interfere with the rational process of Gemini; it can bring doubts and questions which can undermine self-confidence. If this questioning is done in a positive way, however, it is helpful to find Truth.

A spiritual master with Moon and Ketu in Gemini was Ramana Maharshi. As Drupada said when commenting on my Ketu, the master's path was to keep asking "Who am I? Who am I? Who am I?", and keep peeling the onion of identification, of thought-forms, of memories, of associations.

Another spiritual master, Ramakrishna, also described the ego as an onion, made of several layers of self-identifications which contain our soul. When we peel away the form we find the inner purity of consciousness. Ketu is looking at the form and asking what is real and what is not.

Because the ego does not like to be questioned, Ketu with Moon can be difficult, making us dissatisfied and stuck in problem-consciousness. The feelings of Moon become instinctively questioning, and one can have subtle perceptions from people and the environment, which is not always easy, as it is not something we can easily turn off.

Chapter Thirteen

The solution to this sensitivity is to go towards the opposite sign, in my case to Sagittarius. With its gaze fixed towards the universal, Sagittarius for me is like a strong upward flow of energy, where I am not dragged down by any negativity in my environment. It is a work in progress!

Another source of conflict between my Ketu and Moon is that Gemini is my 11th house of community, so it is sociable like Moon, while Ketu is reclusive. If I am in a group of people, I'm only ever completely comfortable if it's spiritual (Ketu), and even then, I'm not the most sociable person. Moon is also my 12th house ruler (spirituality), and it is in the 11th house of community. Again this shows interest in spiritual communities, in fact I am happy when I can spend some time at Ananda, a group of worldwide communities which organizes yoga activities based on the teachings of Yogananda. I also like hatha (physical) yoga courses, where the focus is maybe not as spiritual, but still uplifting. Being active in some way, doing yoga or some sport, is good advice for those with a strong Ketu – if you feel stuck, go do something active, even just physical exercise.

A negative Ketu is rejective of people and even of action. Renunciation, though, is not rejection, but rather the realization that happiness cannot be found outside ourselves. It may be that in certain situations we have to distance ourselves from others, but it is better done with kindness. If we have to be forceful outwardly, it is best to try to still feel kindness inside. A positive Rahu helps us understand that the world is part of God, and we should be kind to everybody.

Rahu and Ketu have two roles in a chart. One role is for Ketu to indicate where we can get stuck due to strong past habits, and for Rahu to indicate what can take us out of that self-limited consciousness. Rahu then shows our sign of growth, and in my chart represents a progressive integration of intuition with an intellect-based perspective. The intellectual side is Ketu in a Mercury sign, while the intuitive side is Rahu in a Jupiter sign. Ketu in Gemini suggests a tendency for excessive rationality, which needs to be balanced by the expansive spiritual enthusiasm of Sagittarius.

Kashiraja's chart

Another role of Rahu and Ketu is to express their own energy as planets: Ketu questions the Moon in a non-intellectual way, requesting new experiential knowledge; Rahu wants more involvement with the 5th house of creative endeavours.

Moon with Ketu, as well as a positive Saturn, can give insight into what is True. That is why both Ketu and Saturn are useful in astrology: Saturn to look at our life with detachment, and Ketu to receive higher insights.

Because Saturn wants us to perceive Truth, it is the planet that brings the most difficult karma. This is explained quite clearly in the words of Asha, a disciple of Yogananda:

"I've noticed an odd fact about karma. If we have a negative tendency, rather than being born into circumstances that will help eradicate it, often we are born into families and conditions that make it *worse*. Until it gets so bad, as I have said about my own journey, that even I notice. In God's infinite mercy, though, that realization seems to come only when our awareness of Him is great enough to give us the wisdom, grace, light, and love to get through it.

Don't, however, in the name of self-honesty become self-centered. Another truth I learned from that first spiritual book was, 'Don't think about yourself and you'll be happy.' At the time, I couldn't conceive of anything but a self-concerned life! I thought I was being spiritual by worrying all the time about whether I was doing well or badly in my efforts to be good!

I used to think that Self-realization meant perfection of the ego. It is a great trick the ego plays on us. The perfection we seek is impossible as long as we remain identified with the ego. Only when we forget the ego-self in the contemplation of God do we find what we are seeking."

Chapter Fourteen

Planets and the Bhagavad Gita

The Bhagavad Gita is the most condensed and profound treatise on yoga. It is, at once, a loose recollection of an historical battle, as well as a description of the conflict between ego and soul. It is narrated as a dialogue between Krishna, who represents Spirit, and Arjuna, the spiritual devotee. Arjuna is the prince commander of the forces of good, and is accompanied by his four brothers: Yudhisthira, Bhima, Nakula and Sahadeva. Sri Yukteswar and Yogananda explained that the five princes are the embodiment of the elements of the five chakras. Each of the princes possesses a conch shell, which represents the astral sound of their chakra; these sounds can be heard at times during meditation.

The eldest brother, Yudhisthira, is the son of Dharma, representing adherence to truth, righteousness, knowledge, wisdom and pure thought; he always spoke the truth and it is said his chariot would hover without touching the earth, symbolizing the transcendence of ether and the divine calmness (pratyahara) of the chakra of Mercury. The conch shell Yudhisthira sounds in battle is Anantavijaya, conqueror of infinity.

The second brother is Bhima, son of Vayu, the deity of air and prana. Just like Hanuman, also a son of Vayu, he has supreme strength, given by control of prana. His conch shell is Paundra, the roar of a lion, a name derived from pund, which means to grind into dust. As we gradually raise our consciousness in meditation, from the lower to the higher chakras, we gain a higher state of spiritual realization. Paundra, in the heart chakra, represents that state, which rules or dissolves the lower states of consciousness.

Being related to Venus, Bhima has a good heart, though occasionally he is depicted as acting emotionally, not thinking everything through. By contrast, Hanuman is closer to Mercury, as he is agile and quick. It is said Bhima could never eat enough to satiate, which represents the impossibility of satisfying the innumerable desires of the heart; it also means that he would stop before feeling full, showing self-control in not pursuing satiety of sense-desires.

The middle brother is Arjuna, the most skillful warrior and commander; he has perfect self-control and humbly obeys Krishna in everything. It is said that, in an earlier time, the two were the twin brothers Nara and Narayan, both incarnations of Vishnu. However, in the Gita Arjuna plays the role of a devotee and Krishna that of guru.

Arjuna is the son of Indra, the king of the gods, and represents fire and the Mars chakra. At the eve of battle, Arjuna asks Krishna why should he fight, since the opposing side is comprised of relatives and childhood friends. This symbolizes the devotee's reluctance at fighting the sense tendencies, which have provided him some form of temporary happiness at various times.

The occasional emotional wavering of a spiritual warrior corresponds to Mars placed in Cancer, contrasted to Mars in Capricorn which has perfect discipline. Cancer is the water sign of the Moon, its focus is personal feelings; it is also inclined to feel a natural sense of kinship with others, it is the sign of mother. Often we'll respond to Mars in Cancer by undermining our resolutions with hesitation, and excessive dwelling in our emotions; thus Cancer is Mars' sign of debilitation. However, it is also possible to blend the energies of Moon and Mars to find a good balance between strength and kindness. The valiant spiritual warrior, having fought the sense tendencies in innumerable battles, both in victory and in defeat, finally subjugates the senses, permanently reestablishing the rule of wisdom. At that point he displays kindness for the senses; they are after all necessary to function on earth. It is when the senses are left to rule that they become harmful.

Another planet that is not easily happy in Cancer is Mercury, our intellect: clarity of reasoning can be confused by excessive emotions. However, like any water sign, Cancer can also enhance Mercury's capacity for intuition.

Arjuna represents asana, self-control, and his conch is Devadatta,

Chapter Fourteen

gift of God, referring to that joy of absorption attained in meditation with a still body and mind.

The youngest two brother princes fighting on the side of Krishna are twins, sons of the twin gods Ashwini. The story of the birth of the Ashwinis continues from that of the birth of Saturn. The Sun, having finally realized that his wife left her shadow as replacement, looks for her in the forest, only to find out she has taken the form of a mare; he turns into a horse and so the Ashwinis are born. They retain their association with the swiftness of their animal symbol, as the Ashwinis are linked to a group of stars placed in the sign of Aries, whose enthusiasm for quickness is akin to racing horses.

Both Nakula and Sahadeva, sons of the Ashwini gods, are described as skilled riders. Nakula, especially, was said to be able to ride a horse so well he could dodge raindrops. Both were also very knowledgeable in astrology, but had different approaches. It is said Nakula would immediately forget any astrological prediction he made, while Sahadeva would keep silent and hid any knowledge he acquired through the stars, as he was forbidden to talk about it. This slight difference reflects their planetary association.

Nakula represents water and Jupiter's chakra, and like the most generous planet he would not keep knowledge for himself; he was also very attractive, the favorite younger brother, loved like Jupiter, the most benefic planet. His conch shell is Sughosha, of sweet and clear sound.

Sahadeva represents earth and Saturn's chakra, and Sahadeva was said to possess all the knowledge of the two planetary teachers, Jupiter and Venus. His deep loyalty to Krishna, and the patience necessary to keep silent about his inner knowledge, are both stable earthy qualities, and certainly remind us of Saturn. Saturn can give deep wisdom, if we overcome the obstacles it gives and become friends with its energy. In the Bhagavad Gita, the dialogue between Krishna and Arjuna represents that between God and all spiritual seekers. Yogananda paraphrases one instance in which Krishna is addressing Arjuna in this way: "It was I who decreed your birth as a mortal being. By your wrong responses to My cosmic delusion, you have imprisoned your soul image in that mortal existence. Your fulfillment lies not in earthly entanglements, but

Planets and the Bhagavad Gita

in Me. Find your Self in Me, which can be done only by removing all obstructions in your path." Saturn is the planet which can help us remove any obstacle in our path.

The conch of Sahadeva is Manipushpaka, display of sound, symbolizing the earth level and material manifestation. The material creation is manifested when light progressively slows down its vibrations into ether, air, fire, water and earth. Conversely, to return our consciousness to the light, we have to spiritualize each successive element and raise our energy through the chakras. Sri Krishna symbolizes the light at the spiritual eye, in the 6th chakra, and his conch is Panchajanya, manifesting (ja) the five (pancha) elements.

Chapter Fifteen

Adelle's chart

Water is a flowing, receptive element. It is the element most closely associated with feelings, which are the receptive part of our consciousness. Receptivity, though, does not equate to passivity: we choose the focus of our feelings. It is important to be aware of this focus, as it may be influenced by subconscious habits, whether positive or negative. If we focus on the negative things in our life, water can become too emotional, and the lack of emotional clarity and calmness will just produce unhappiness. Dramatic and upsetting emotions can become a habit, something we feel is normal, but it is not. Still water reflections are clear. Emotions, when calm, become intuitive feelings.

This is true for all water signs, but especially for Scorpio, as it is ruled by fiery Mars. It is also true when Moon and Saturn are together, because Saturn's intention is to teach self-control to the Moon.

A good example is Adelle's chart, who has Moon and Saturn in Scorpio.

In her chart the ascendant is Taurus, and Venus is in Aquarius in the 10th house. Venus in the 10th house shows that public work is important to her, while the placement in Aquarius means that she is interested in knowledge, and in using that knowledge to help others. The ruler of Aquarius is Saturn, which is in the 7th house, so her primary interest is knowledge relating to people, like counselling or medicine.

By contrast, my ascendant ruler is in the 9th house, a house of knowledge, and the 9th ruler is in the 7th house, so it is somewhat similar to her Venus in Aquarius and Saturn in the 7th house. However, my ascendant ruler is in Aries, not Aquarius. Aries is more like a child self-absorbed in playing and finding out how things work, while Aquarius is naturally oriented to others. Both charts show interest in applying knowledge to help other people, but in my chart there is also an evident drive to acquire knowledge even if not directly practical, the kind of drive that motivated me to study physics.

Aquarius, as a sign, is impersonal, however Venus is not an impersonal planet. Similarly, Saturn, an impersonal planet, is with debilitated Moon in Scorpio, a personal planet in a personal sign. As a consequence, the impersonal character of Aquarius and Saturn are not evident in Adelle. In fact, in her chart Scorpio's influence is dominant over that of Aquarius.

Scorpio is a focal point because of the Moon, and because it is opposite the ascendant. Such a combination in the 7th house of relationships is likely to attract dramatic situations in our relationships, romantic and not. A relationship that could be especially involved is with her parents, because Saturn and Moon in her chart symbolize her parents.

In any chart, Sun symbolizes father, and Moon the mother. Planets have certain meanings always associated with them. A positive Moon gives happiness of mind, like a mother to her child. A positive Sun gives strength and confidence, like a father. Moon and Sun, then, symbolize the parents in all charts. In a specific chart, we will also consider the rulers of the 9th and 10th house for father, and the 4th house for mother. In Adelle's chart, then, Sun represents her mother, and Saturn her father.

Saturn, Sun and Moon together show different characteristics of Adelle's parents; note how two of these planets are in Scorpio.

An immature response to the depth of Scorpio in the 7th house can turn our life into a drama. The key is to be aware of whether we are actively participating in that drama, or learning that participation is not mandatory. A mature response is depth of understanding and friendship, in all relationships.

If we find ourselves in a difficult situation, it is challenging, but essential, to understand that it is our inborn tendencies which have attracted it. By changing the way we respond to such difficult situations, we will stop making them worse, and start attracting positive experiences instead. To respond with wisdom, we need

Chapter Fifteen

to take a step back and avoid reacting instinctively; we need a minimum amount of detachment to begin to understand what is really happening.

Saturn represents detachment, which is not too easily attained in a Mars' sign, but it is important to find happiness. Once we start practising it in Scorpio, we will be able to become intuitive and insightful. By contrast, if Saturn were with Moon in Libra, the sign of Saturn's exaltation, we would be more inclined to not fall into emotional and difficult situations. Though, our capacity to get into troubles is not easily stopped by any one planetary placement.

In any case, Scorpio looks beneath the surface, and can indicate a serious search for happiness in inner life. In fact, Adelle started practising yoga and meditation at a relatively young age. Saturn rules her 9th house of spirituality, so it can have a positive influence, with a calm Moon. How can we calm our mind? Yogananda said

Me Ju Ra	Su	Ma	
Ve			
	Mo Sa		Ke

Adelle's chart. Venus, the ascendant ruler, has strength from being in the 10th house. When a planet is underlined, like Saturn in Scorpio, it means it is retrograde.

that our thoughts are universally, not individually rooted; they originate not in ourselves, but in the universe. We choose the thoughts we want to attune with. This may sound alarming to the ego, as if negating the very existence of our personality, but

Adelle's chart

the point is that it shouldn't sound alarming to *us*: we are not our ego, we are the soul. Those who have strong water signs are instinctively aware of the mind's ability to pick up thoughts and feelings, like a radio.

This is especially true in Adelle's chart, as she has five planets in water signs: Moon and Saturn in Scorpio, and Jupiter, Rahu and Mercury in Pisces.

Mercury in Pisces can be very intuitive, if occasionally not too attentive. Virgo and Pisces, when balanced, are intuitive; they show capacity for discrimination, which is intuitive intellect, and insightful feelings. When unbalanced, Virgo can make us excessively focused on details, and Pisces excessively open to feelings.

Virgo can obsess over details, while Mercury in debilitation can lack focus. I'm not trying to hedge my interpretation: excessive focus or complete lack thereof are opposite ends of an unbalanced swinging scale. The key is to have the insight of knowing when details are important, and when they can be ignored.

Pisces and Virgo are especially important for Adelle's chart because of Rahu and Ketu. Ketu in Virgo shows skillful attention to details. In fact, Adelle has worked in a laboratory doing detailed scientific experiments.

Considering that Mercury is in Pisces, however, Ketu in Virgo can also give obsessive focus on details as well as a momentary loss of rationality. I remember once, when she was cleaning the steering wheel of her car with some solvent, and the cloth kept coming out black as if dirty, so she kept using more solvent. I mentioned to her that the solvent was stripping the paint, but she only stopped when she finally realized the wheel had become a lighter shade of grey.

Another consequence of Mercury's debilitation and Ketu in Virgo is sensitivity to physical things – Virgo is the mutable earth sign. For example, she has a mild allergy to pollen and a sensitive stomach. Jupiter strengthens Mercury, so she doesn't actually have

Chapter Fifteen

any food allergies. However, we don't need to look at a chart to know these things, I mention it only as another example of how the stars reflect actual experiences.

In any case, Pisces, the 11th house of community, is evidently stronger thanks to Jupiter. Together with Scorpio in the 7th, this shows meaningful friendships, something certainly true for her. Lahiri Mahasaya also had Rahu in the 11th house and he was present in the lives of many people. Although, Adelle is more comfortable with a few friends at a time rather than big groups, because her Moon is in Scorpio. Scorpio wants deep friendships, but not in large social groups.

Jupiter in Pisces also shows a gift for subtle perception and understanding, as well as compassion and caring for others. Jupiter is a good balance for her influential Saturn, because any difficulty always becomes worse when we focus too much on ourselves, especially when Saturn is with the Moon. Saturn with Moon can make us contract in ourselves, while Jupiter in Pisces expands our perceptions.

We shouldn't forget, though, that Saturn and Jupiter need to be balanced. Although Jupiter and Pisces are a good influence on Saturn and Scorpio, that influence can go slightly astray.

Specifically, for Taurus ascendants Saturn rules the benefic 9th house, while Jupiter the 8th and 11th; by house rulership alone, Saturn is more benefic. Saturn represents duty, and here it also rules the 10th house of public work and duty. Energetically, Saturn has strength from being in the 7th house, but Jupiter is stronger in this chart, being in own sign.

Although it is great to have a strong Jupiter, for Adelle it rules the 11th house, a kama house, and one meaning of kama is desires. Similarly, Saturn is in a kama house in Scorpio, a sign which can be very attracted to desires. The consequence is that if Jupiter steers the wrong way, Saturn might follow. If Saturn were in a less personal sign, for example in Capricorn, then its restraining influence would be more stable. In Scorpio, Saturn can lose its detachment.

Just like Scorpio, Pisces is in a kama house. Pisces is mutable water, the most easily influenced sign of the zodiac, and in this chart it is occupied by potentially disruptive planets. Apart from Jupiter, in Pisces we find Rahu, who likes the flux and change of world involvement, and Mercury, which can be a bit irrational when debilitated.

With such planetary combinations, there is a definite possibility for Saturn's restraint to be overruled, because of some mischief happening in Scorpio and Pisces. When Saturn's discipline becomes unreliable, we should be careful to not fall into the temptation of irresponsibility, like excessive shopping or avoiding our duty in life, and in general feeling that we'll find happiness by realizing our material desires.

In any case, this is a secondary interpretation. The primary indication of the planets in Pisces and Scorpio is a talent for understanding others, compassion, kindness and generosity – all qualities Adelle possesses. Her intuition, a water quality, can be impressive, even in small things. For example, a couple of times she pointed at a street out of sight and told me she felt there was a citrus tree there. We went to check: once we found a mandarin tree, and another time it was an orange tree.

Another quite evident characteristic of Adelle is that, although she has a lot of water in her chart, she is also quite willful. That can be seen from Mars, which is influential on the ascendant, and from her exalted Sun. Taurus, being fixed earth, also tends to be rather unmovable. The fact that she has strong water signs, however, means that she is more inclined to balance will and receptivity, compared to a fiery chart like mine, which has no planet in water signs.

In her case, the Sun is in the 12th house of spirituality, and rules the 4th house of inner happiness: a good placement for a yogi. It also makes the Sun slightly less prominent: in my chart it rules the ascendant so its strength is more central. The Sun represents physical vitality and its strength offsets some of the weakness of her Virgo, the mutable earth sign, however, being in the 12th house, the Sun is more oriented to spiritual rather than

Chapter Fifteen

physical expression.

Coming back to Saturn in the 7th house, there is something important to remember, for those with this planet in an influential position: to relax. Saturn can give a strong tendency of worrying, which attracts only unhappiness, not solutions. To counteract that, it is best to start a habit of inner contentment and generosity. In Adelle's chart Saturn and Moon are together opposite Taurus. Saturn is a planet with a serious purpose and a drive to achieve perfection. Taurus is also an achiever, because of its determination. The Moon rules the 4th house of inner happiness, and it is in Scorpio with Saturn, so it can forget the peace of inner contentment in constant search of perfection. But perfection is not of this world, and our soul is already perfect, so why all this struggle? We can make a choice, every moment, to be happy. It may not work always, or even at all, in the beginning, but, if we keep trying to live in happiness, we will find that we are happier every day. With happiness, we'll find that we can confront any problem with a much better attitude, until we will stop attracting problems altogether.

Worrying and constantly struggling to achieve something is the opposite attitude, which says "I cannot be happy until I've solved this problem, or achieved this goal." But there's always some other problem or goal afterward, and happiness gets forgotten on the way. If we live happiness first, then we will have endless energy to achieve anything. Yogananda said that if we attune our will to God, nothing is impossible.

Even in small things, masters have that power. When Yogananda was living in Los Angeles, sometimes a disciple, Oliver, would drive him around. Once, he asked Oliver to get ready to go during a torrential rain. Oliver thought it an odd request, but in a few minutes went outside anyway. The sun was shining, the ground impossibly dry, and Yogananda said smiling: "For you, Oliver."

Sometimes Saturn or Taurus can make us work too hard, then we need to remember the need for relaxation and receptivity. Continuously pressuring ourselves too much can make us feel discouraged, and it will prevent us from doing our best. Neither should we swing in the opposite direction and be lazy, we need to find balance.

Adelle's chart

Mars in Taurus can become too fixed, and then we might fall into a habit of procrastination. It can be quite frustrating to know you are supposed to do something, but keep putting it off. Inner happiness is the key to change this self-defeating habit. If we make an effort to uplift our energy and live with inner contentment, we won't shy away from doing anything that is our responsibility.

Yogananda said: "There are no such things as obstacles: there are only opportunities!"

Kriyananda has appropriately commented on those words: "This teaching of my Guru's might well be engraved over the exit of every home. Obstacles challenge one to summon up more energy in oneself. Without them, people would become lethargic. Indeed, even the worst karma can be a blessing, in the sense that it prods you toward self-improvement."

It can be difficult to face obstacles while remaining happy, but a positive attitude will attract positive things. It is a spiritual law – it will come true.

Chapter Sixteen

Planetary friendships

Planets can support or obstruct each other, depending on how we respond to the interaction of their energies. For example, Saturn is discipline and contraction, Jupiter expansion and prosperity. If we are able to balance them, the two planets will support each other. But if they are unbalanced, Saturn can constrict Jupiter's inspiration, or Jupiter could disrupt Saturn's discipline by being too open to unwholesome influences. Although, it is more likely for Saturn to create problems, as Jupiter is generally more benefic.

Planets in the same sign have the strongest interaction; the closer they are to each other, the stronger their interaction. Another important connection is between a planet and the ruler of the sign it occupies. Planets are immediately harmonious with some signs, while with others some effort is required to bring together the combination of energies. Astrologers often refer to this as friendship: some planets are friends with certain planets and are generally comfortable in their signs, while they may be neutral or even enemies with other planets, indicating some disharmony to be resolved.

In general, planets in friendly signs are stronger than when in neutral or enemy signs, however it also depends on other factors, like house placement. Of course, if a planet is exalted or in own sign, then it will always have strength.

Planetary friendships are loosely based on two groups: Saturn, Venus and Mercury, which rule air and earth signs; and Sun, Moon, Jupiter and Mars, which rule water and fire. With a few exceptions, planets will be friends with their own elemental group and not with the other. No planet considers the ruler of its exaltation sign an enemy, and no planet considers one of its neighboring planets an enemy – if they are not friends, they will be

Planetary friendships

neutral. Neighboring planets rule adjacent signs in the zodiac. For example, Mars' signs, Aries and Scorpio, are adjacent to the signs of Jupiter and Venus, which are then Mars' neighboring planets.

Five of the planets, Saturn, Jupiter, Mars, Venus, and Sun, follow the exact same rule: they consider the planets of their elemental group as friends, and those of the other group as enemies. All five planets are neutral to the neighboring planet which belongs to the other elemental group. Two of these planets, Mars and Venus, are exalted in a sign ruled by the other elemental group, so they consider that ruler neutral, instead of an enemy.

For example, Jupiter rules water (Pisces) and fire (Sagittarius), so it takes as friends the planets which rule water or fire: Sun, Moon and Mars. It regards as neutral its neighbor Saturn, which otherwise would be its enemy. The reason for the neighboring planet rule is probably that adjacent signs have slightly closer interaction, which can improve their harmony – to a degree.

To summarize, Jupiter is in a sign of a friend when in the signs of Sun, Moon or Mars, and it will have strength there. It is in a neutral sign in Capricorn or Aquarius, and it will have less strength. Capricorn is its debilitation sign, but Aquarius, although neutral, can actually be a good placement for Jupiter, as it is a sign of wisdom. Jupiter is in the sign of an enemy in the signs of Mercury and Venus, and it will have less strength than in Aquarius, but more than in Capricorn.

Strength by sign is not everything: Jupiter in a neutral or enemy sign can still be a benefic influence in a chart. We just need to understand the specific interaction, in that chart, between sign and planet. For example, Jupiter in Taurus, an enemy earthy sign, may be more focused on expanding our material desires, but that is not a given. Taurus is a gentle sign. With a little effort, we could be expansive and kind, and be a stable refuge for friends to seek comfort. Similarly, Jupiter in Gemini, another enemy sign, may be too focused on rationality, something not entirely agreeable with the planet of inspiration. However, it could also indicate an expansive and inspired intellect.

Conversely, a planet in the sign of a friend is not necessarily always positive. Planetary friendship can give a rough idea of

Chapter Sixteen

how much strength a planet has in a sign, and can be helpful in the interpretation, but it is not a crucial concept. Our actions and free will can strengthen or weaken a planet, and much also depends on how we use that strength.

Following the same rule, Saturn considers Venus and Mercury as friends, Jupiter neutral, and Sun, Moon and Mars as enemies. We have already seen how Saturn can have conflicts with its inimical planets.

Sun is friends with Moon, Mars and Jupiter, it considers Mercury neutral and Saturn and Venus as enemies.

Mars considers Moon, Jupiter and Sun friends, Saturn and Venus neutral, and Mercury an enemy.

Venus takes Mercury and Saturn as friends, Mars and Jupiter as neutral, and Sun and Moon as enemies.

It is more important to understand the underlying reasons for these friendships than to actually remember all of them. For example, we already mentioned how Mars, the planet of action, is not immediately comfortable in Virgo, a thinking sign. However, this is only their initial interaction, we can develop any planetary relationship into a friendship.

For Mercury and Moon the friendships are not based on their elemental group. Mercury considers the Sun and Venus as friends and the other planets neutral, except for the Moon which it sees as an enemy. The Moon considers the Sun and Mercury as friends, and all other planets neutral.

Why Mercury and Moon behave differently? The two elemental groups speak different languages, air and earth, water and fire, so it is understandable that some energy is lost trying to communicate with the other group. I think part of the reason Mercury does not follow this rule is that it is somewhat different, elementally; its chakra is ether, transcending the elements, and it is exalted in its own sign. However, Mercury, being smart, probably realizes that everybody needs friends. The Sun makes Mercury bright, so it is a natural choice for a friend. Now, if we imagine the ideal

Planetary friendships

Mercury enjoying some of its favorite activities, like acquiring knowledge, reflecting on ideas, spending time with friends, or reading a book, we get a happy picture of relaxed focus. I think this is its natural link to Venus, especially to Taurus who likes relaxation. Jupiter, the other benefic teacher, also appreciates knowledge, but Mercury is half Moon, half Jupiter. Compared to Jupiter, it is more involved in the material world and does not share right away the spiritual enthusiasm of Jupiter. Venus, on the other hand, is more involved in the material world. Probably that is why Mercury considers Venus a friend and Jupiter neutral.

The only enemy of Mercury is the Moon, because it can be emotional and cloud Mercury's mental clarity.

As for the Moon's friendships, it is the most adaptable planet; it may have difficulties with Saturn, but Moon is gentle so it has no enemies. Moon and Sun symbolize Divine Mother and Father, so they are friends. I think one reason it considers Mercury a friend is that Moon is our state of mind, and it is naturally attracted to happiness and calmness – Mercury gives clarity of mind, which is conducive to both.

Moon obviously likes Taurus, its sign of exaltation. As to Libra, Kriyananda notes how it can become, paradoxically, the least balanced of all signs as its search for inner harmony can make it run from one extreme to the other. Moon, if emotional, will not be happy with such lack of balance. Perhaps that is why, overall, it considers Venus neutral rather than a friend.

Note how the friendships are not always reciprocal: for example Mars considers Mercury an enemy, while Mercury considers Mars neutral. This means that Mercury in a Mars sign will have a bit more strength than Mars in a Mercury sign – though house placement could change that.

In any case, I find it easier to understand how a planet relates to a sign or another planet by reflecting on a specific chart, without thinking too much of these rules, but planetary friendships can be an aid to intuition.

For an easy reference, it's easy to remember that all planets, except Moon and Mercury, are stronger in a sign of their elemental group. Moon is stronger in the signs of Sun and Mercury, while

Chapter Sixteen

Mercury in the signs of Sun and Venus. Planets are always stronger in their own sign or if exalted.

The chart of Lahiri Mahasaya is a good example of a strong chart with planets in enemy signs: Jupiter in Libra, Venus in Leo and Saturn in Cancer. Those planets have become friends with their enemies through the spiritual effort of the exalted yogi. It is interesting that his Jupiter is in a Venus sign and he was a householder. Venus is the teacher of those who still have desires, like getting married. Lahiri Mahasaya, as a spiritual master, had no personal desire, but for our benefit he exemplified how to be a yogi while having a family. His Saturn, in Cancer, has spiritualized every trait of that sign, creating a welcoming home to wisdom seekers. Similarly, his Venus in Leo expresses the highest trait of the Sun sign, shining its light on everyone.

Chapter Seventeen

The stars in each moment

On a bright sunny day, with a deep blue sky and wandering white clouds, some people will be happy for the weather and go relax at the beach, others will be in a bad mood and not even notice. At any one time, the stars are in the same position for a lot of people. Unless a planet is right at the end of a sign, only the ascendant changes as we travel around the Earth.

Mars in Leo is objectively different from Mars in Virgo, but the response to Mars' placement will be unique for each person, though sharing some general characteristics. As I was writing this, Mars moved from Leo into Virgo and I resumed my practice of hatha yoga, which I had neglected for quite some time. Mars is the planet of action and Virgo is the sign of practical techniques like physical yoga. I've done hatha yoga plenty of times in the past, regardless of Mars' placement, but it is true that sometimes you can see subtle changes reflected in the stars, such as this.

The stars change constantly, and at any time we can look at the chart for that moment to explain what is happening. Looking is like asking a question, to which we receive an answer through our intuition. That is why astrology is both a science and an art: we need a scientific, technical understanding of the objective part of astrology, and a capacity to listen to intuition, through attunement to inner guidance.

During each day the planets normally remain in the same sign, maybe one or two will move at most, but the ascendant is different every couple of hours, and so the houses change rather frequently. Sometimes the change is quite evident: one time I was studying astrology but I was getting tired, then suddenly I felt a surge of energy – the ascendant had just changed from Sagittarius to Capricorn. When the ascendant was Sagittarius, its ruler,

Chapter Seventeen

Jupiter, was in Taurus in the 6th house, with Venus and Ketu: by sign and house not too strong, though it received energy from Venus. Although a negative Ketu could block Jupiter somewhat, for studying astrology it was a good combination.

However, for Capricorn ascendant, Saturn was exalted in Libra in the 10th house, a much stronger placement for the ascendant ruler: I felt energized. Energy in the 10th house can be used for good or bad. Saturn's strength was good for the ascendant, but it wasn't necessarily so for the other planet in Libra, the Moon. After a while I got into an overly critical frame of mind – the influence of Saturn on the Moon. Some time later, though, suddenly I started to calm down; I checked the chart again and the ascendant had just changed to Aquarius. Now Saturn and Moon were in the 9th house, a more benevolent influence. I cannot always feel the influence of the stars so clearly. However, when we are not able to find a full correspondence between the chart of that moment and what we are experiencing, it is not necessarily because we are not good enough – maybe our aura is strong and we are partly outside the influence of the stars.

It can be practical to choose an appropriate astrological time to do something important. I deliberately did not get married on a Saturday, but on Friday, day of Venus; another good day would be Thursday.

As a detailed example, once I was writing a section of this book, something about interiorization of the mind and Mercury, and I wanted to insert a chart. I looked at the chart for that moment and found that the ascendant was Virgo, a good sign for writing about practical techniques for a yogi. Virgo is attentive to details and I wanted to add a detail.

In the chart for that moment, Mercury is debilitated, but the good thing is that in Pisces it can have a great capacity for intuition, and the fact that it is opposite the ascendant strengthens Virgo to some degree. Mercury also draws some energy, through Pisces, from Jupiter, which is in the sign of a friend with exalted Sun.

The 8th house is strong, a good thing for writing about astrology, as it is a house interested in deep metaphysical things. Astrology, like yoga, is both practical and metaphysical.

The stars in each moment

Me	Su Ju	Ke Ve	
			Mo
			Ma
	Ra	S̲a̲	/

A chart for a moment. The ascendant ruler is not strong, but receives some energy from Jupiter, the ruler of Pisces, which is in the sign of a friend, Mars, with another friend, exalted Sun.

Venus, as the 9th ruler in the 9th house, is in an excellent placement as it is a benefic teacher planet; it is in Taurus, and my intention is to write a book that is a warm read, not dryly intellectual.

Ketu can be intuitive and is interested in spiritual knowledge, so it is happy in the 9th house.

Rahu is in the 3rd house of motivated energy and writing – in Scorpio which is similar to the 8th house. Saturn is retrograde, looking for Truth within, and exalted; it rules the benefic 5th house. Moon is in own sign, in the 11th house of gains and community, and I was home doing something productive with the intention of being helpful to others as well. Mars is the ruler of the 3rd and 8th houses, and is in the 12th house: my energy was directed to a spiritual purpose while in relative isolation – 12th house of seclusion and spirituality tied to the houses of writing and astrology.

The chart is also good if read from the Moon and Sun, a fact we can use as a confirmation of our initial interpretation. It can be useful to read a chart not only from the ascendant, but also from the Moon, that is taking it as a new ascendant and considering its sign as the new 1st house. This will give a special perspective from the point of view of our mind, and show how we feel about our circumstances. The same can be done from the Sun, because it represents our soul, and, similarly to the 1st house, self-confidence and vitality.

Read from the Moon, the ascendant becomes Cancer, which is strong because the Moon rules and occupies it. The ruler of the 3rd house of writing is now in the 9th house, connecting their meanings. Rahu is in the 5th house, using intelligence for a practical purpose, and Ketu is in the 11th house, spiritual gains. Writing certainly fits both houses, as it has benefited me spiritually. The 8th ruler is exalted and retrograde, excellent for writing about astrology.

Reading from the Sun, the ascendant is Aries, strong because of Sun's exaltation. The ascendant ruler, Mars, is in the benefic 5th house, in the sign of an exalted friend; Mars also rules the 8th house. Jupiter, the planet of wisdom, expansion and spiritual subjects, is on the ascendant. Exalted Saturn aspects it. Now, in general, Saturn can bring difficulties, especially to the Sun, but it is exalted, so slightly less problematic because softened by Venus' sign.

Saturn also rules a trine from the normal ascendant. That's something we can keep in mind to understand if there is mutual support between the three ascendants of any chart: the normal ascendant, Moon and Sun. Most importantly, though, Saturn shows power of concentration and discipline, necessary to write a good book, so it is a good influence on Aries.

Continuing from the point of view of the Sun ascendant, Rahu in the 8th house is also good in this case, because this is not the chart of a person, but a chart for a specific purpose, in a certain moment. An activity like writing about an 8th house subject, done under the influence of Rahu in Scorpio, is quite different from having your natal chart with the same placement. For a limited time and with a specific focus, we might find it easier to find a good response to some planetary placement, while if it is in our natal chart we probably need more practice.

Overall, an excellent time to be writing but I didn't choose it deliberately, I was writing because I felt inspired.

Chapter Eighteen

Signs and the Bhavagad Gita

One verse of the Gita names twelve warriors on the side of Krishna, listing them together with Bhima and Arjuna, the most valiant of the five prince brothers. It is tempting to think they symbolize the twelve signs, but even if it were not true, it's still a good imagination exercise to reflect on which warrior corresponds to which sign.

Yogananda has commented on that Gita verse, explaining that each of these twelve metaphysical warriors represents a yoga concept described by Patanjali. Yogananda also derived a metaphorical meaning for them, from the sanskrit roots of their names. I also mention some additional hints taken from a translation of the Gita commentaries of Sri Yukteswar and Lahiri Mahasaya; although I cannot attest to their accuracy, they are consistent with Yogananda's information and with my interpretation. The choice of which sign corresponds to which warrior is often quite clear, though for a few there are alternative choices. This puzzle has only twelve pieces, however, and I believe the following is the best way to arrange them.

1. *Dhristaketu* represents the power of mental resistance, yama, so he should be either Capricorn or Aquarius, which are the signs of the 1st chakra of yama. Dhristaketu's name means to uphold dharma and overcome adversities through discriminative intellect, so he must be *Aquarius*, an air sign. Swami Sri Yukteswar had Jupiter and Moon in Aquarius. The perfect example of an expansive Aquarian nature, he was impersonal yet kind. Jupiter shows his expansive spiritual wisdom, while Moon inspired his kindness – detached because in Aquarius. Aquarius represented his impersonal discriminative intellect, dedicated to destroying ignorance in anybody who sought his help. Yogananda said that

109

Chapter Eighteen

one of the most important things Sri Yukteswar taught was to learn to behave, a rather appropriate example of yama and of Dhristaketu.

2. *Shaibya* is the power of mental adherence, niyama, which makes him either Sagittarius or Pisces. The root of his name is the same as Shiva's, and it means in whom all things lie, reminding us of the all-encompassing *Pisces*. Shiva also means auspicious and happy, like joyful Sagittarius, however the metaphorical meaning of Shaibya is adherence to what is beneficial – the spiritual prescriptions of niyama. Adherence to niyama first requires receptivity, and of the two Jupiter signs, Pisces is the most receptive. It is said that Rabindranath Tagore, the Indian poet and Nobel-prize winner, whom Yogananda recounts meeting in his autobiography, had Moon and ascendant in Pisces. He's been quoted as saying: "Everything comes to us that belongs to us if we create the capacity to receive it." His receptivity to inspiration came from his practice of niyama, like contentment, introspection, and spiritual devotion, the strengths of Shaibya.

3. *Kuntibhoja* is asana, self-control. He represents dispassion towards the unreasonable requests of the body, fiercely fighting against laziness, restlessness and sense-attachment. With its fiery willfulness it is closer to *Aries* than watery Scorpio.

4. *Yudhamanyu* is pranayama, control of life-force. His name means to fight with great zeal and determination. Libra is the active air sign, while Taurus is fixed earth. The sustaining energy and determination of *Taurus* is needed to fight the continuous allure of the material world to draw our life-force outwardly. Krishna has Moon and ascendant in Taurus, and during his life he valiantly fights many times for dharma, yet he refuses to yield any weapon in the important battle narrated in the Bhagavad Gita. Krishna only drives Arjuna's chariot and acts as his counsellor – why? There are many reasons, but the relevant one here is that he stands in stark contrast with all the warriors, on the side of good and bad, who are all convinced to be on the rightful side. In that way, Krishna reminds us that inner determination, guided by the soul's intuition, is superior to mere outward commitments, which can be misguided even with the best intentions. The intuitive control

Signs and the Bhavagad Gita

of life-force in our efforts is the strength of Yudhamanyu.

5. *Purujit* is pratyahara, interiorization. The interiorization of life-force brings a steady mental calmness, which is better supported by the etheric-earth stability of *Virgo* rather than the etheric-air adaptability of Gemini. For the same reason Mercury is exalted in Virgo, not Gemini.

Yogananda had Saturn, the ruler of the 6th house of obstacles, in Virgo. When living in Los Angeles he had a few physical accidents that would have incapacitated a normal man. In such occasions he demonstrated perfect control of his life-force: when he'd let it flow outwardly, he'd grimace in pain; when he'd direct it inwardly, he was innerly free of any discomfort.

Lahiri Mahasaya had Rahu and Sun in Virgo, and after a full workday as an accountant, he would remain in samadhi all night, undisturbed by the surrounding disciples.

6. *Saubhadra* represents samyama, which means holding together. Samyama groups together the three concepts of concentration, meditation and samadhi – it represents an intense state of absorption on the object of concentration. Saubhadra is *Cancer* because of the focalizing power of that sign, which can become intensely absorbed and attentive; that is why Cancer can be the most personal and attached sign of the zodiac, but also the most caring and attentive, like a mother. If highly spiritual, Cancer can see the whole universe as its own, just like in samadhi.

Sri Yukteswar refers to samadhi as true concentration. The energy center of concentration is the spiritual eye, which corresponds to Leo, but Cancer also can indicate concentration, with its capacity to become fully absorbed on what interests it.

Yogananda explains that Saubhadra represents the self-mastery which bestows light or illumination.

He often stated that our consciousness is normally centered at the energy center at the medulla oblongata, the seat of the ego, which corresponds to Cancer. Gradually, a yogi shifts the focus of his consciousness to the spiritual eye in the forehead, which corresponds to Leo. I think the process of samyama, from concentration to the light of samadhi, parallels the move from Cancer to Leo, reinforcing the choice of Cancer for Saubhadra.

Chapter Eighteen

7. *Yuyudhana* is shraddha, divine devotion, so he could be Pisces, the sign of universal empathy and compassion. Pisces has a natural openness that makes it easier to feel devotion. An alternative is Libra, in the heart chakra. Yudh means to fight, and Sri Yukteswar describes Yuyudhana as the desire to practice kriya, the meditative yoga technique which actively uplifts the life-force in our energetic spine. This makes it closer to *Libra*, the active air sign with a strong desire for inner harmony, rather than Pisces, which is more passive.

Sri Yukteswar refers both Yuyudhana and Yudhamanyu to kriya yoga and the expansion of consciousness into infinity, supporting the idea that they are linked to the same chakra and are both signs of Venus.

8. *Uttamaujas* is virya, vital celibacy, referring to the use of the life-force for spiritual rather than sensual purposes. This suggests a Jupiter sign, in the 2nd chakra, the chakra linked to the reproductive organs. Another possibility would be a Venus sign, in the heart chakra of pranayama, control of the life-force.

Considering that ojas, part of Uttamaujas' name, means energy and power, Uttamaujas is probably Sagittarius, a fire sign. This translation, though, is not conclusive by itself, because a different translation links Uttamaujas to Venus instead of Jupiter. It is common for sanskrit words to have multiple related meanings, to convey a subtle concept in different ways.

Ojas is power and virya means courage, while the sanskrit name of Venus, Shukra, means resplendent. However, each of these three terms can also indicate the bright vital essence that empowers a yogi who practices celibacy.

The uncertainty between Venus and Jupiter is resolved because Lahiri Mahasaya refers to Uttamaujas as Shakti, while Sri Yukteswar translates it as fiery vigor. This makes it *Sagittarius*, a fire sign whose chakra deity is Shakti. In *The holy science*, Sri Yukteswar says virya is moral courage, a parallel meaning to vital celibacy, as we need courage to resist sensual habits.

9. *Chekitana* is smriti, spiritual memory, and his name means intelligent. *Gemini* is the natural association for this warrior. Spiritual memory is the ability to remember our true soul nature. Mercury

Signs and the Bhavagad Gita

signs are in the ether chakra, and ether is where patterns of energy are stored, like blueprints to be used for material manifestation. In this sense ether acts like a place to store information, a spiritual memory. The more we remember our true nature, the more we perceive the innate presence of Spirit in everyone, in fact Gemini is a sociable sign.

Swami Kriyananda has a Gemini ascendant, and he acts as a memory for all of us, recollecting for our benefit the teachings of Yogananda in their purest form. How many stories has he narrated to us from the times they spent together, and how many books has he written, thanks to his intuitive memory of Yogananda's words!

10. *Virata* is samadhi. His name means to be immersed in the inner Self. *Scorpio* is the natural association as it can be strong and self-possessed. Virata was a king who ruled in the Matsya kingdom, and matsya means fish, suggesting a water sign. Matsya was the first avatar of Vishnu, a giant fish who saved the progenitor of mankind, Manu, from a great flood. Scorpio is a fixed (Vishnu) water sign. Before the events narrated in the Bhagavad Gita, Arjuna and his four brothers spend a year hidden in disguise at the court of King Virata. Of all the signs of the zodiac, Scorpio is certainly the most secretive.

11. *Kashiraja* is prajna, discriminative intelligence. Kashi means shining and raj means to shine and to rule. Kashi is a name for Varanasi, or Benares, the most ancient holy city in India, so Kashiraja in a way also means king of Kashi. The metaphorical meaning, though, is shining, causing other things to shine and be revealed – in other words, insight. For a while I thought that Kashiraja was Aries, until I realized it is actually Leo. I was misled by the fact that I have exalted Sun and Mercury in Aries, so my perception of Aries had a strong Sun quality. When studying astrology, we have to be detached, or our own chart can bias our understanding. Kashiraja means to reign with light, in a brilliant way, so it clearly indicates *Leo*, the royal sign of the zodiac.

12. *Drupada* is tivra-samvega, extreme dispassion – surely a sign of Saturn. Pada means step, and the whole name means stepping swiftly. Kriyananda comments on how the symbol of Capricorn is a strange animal, half goat and half fish; the goat in India is

Chapter Eighteen

substituted for an antelope but both indicate sure-footedness. To step swiftly, metaphorically, means to be detached and not be side-tracked by various passing interests. *Capricorn* is active and detached, a good fit for the meaning of Drupada.

Much knowledge has been lost from the time of the Bhagavad Gita, and only a master yogi could really assert the truth of the association between these twelve warriors and the signs. However, it is certainly possible that they each had a sign particularly strong, similarly to Arjuna and his four brothers, who each expressed the energy of a different planet and chakra.

Chapter Nineteen

Kate's chart

We have already seen three examples of Libra ascendants, all of socially active people who are dedicated to helping others. Perhaps it is easier to meet Librans because they are involved in society, in fact I have another such example. *Kate is a Libra and she fulfills Libra's call of social involvement. It is interesting that for Libra the ascendant ruler also rules the 8th house of transformation, and all the Libra ascendants mentioned in this book actively help others to transform their lives. Aries is the only other ascendant linked in such a way to the 8th house, and it also likes change, being the sign of beginning and initiative.

The difference is that Aries is an independent fiery sign while Libra is an idealistic air sign. Venus, the lovely planet of joy and beauty, is generally more benefic than Mars so it is easier for Libra to become involved in social transformation, while Aries is more focused on changing itself or its immediate personal circumstances. If Aries becomes socially involved, then it'd probably prefer a revolutionary approach, not diplomatic.

Kate, like Lahiri Mahasaya, has Rahu in Virgo. Additionally, her Venus is not in Leo but in Virgo, together with Mars – this makes Virgo a central focus. The primary energy of the chart will be a mixture of Libra and Virgo.

Because of the emphasis on the 12th house of renunciation and spirituality, and the strength of her exalted Jupiter, it is not surprising that Kate is a yoga and meditation teacher. Together with *Shifu she is the Ananda leader of a small European country. For financial support they also teach english as well as martial arts like tai chi. Jupiter is also strong because it is in the 10th house of public work, and it represents a strong protection and spiritual blessing.

Chapter Nineteen

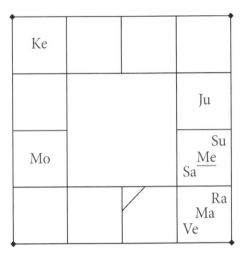

Kate's chart. Venus, the ascendant ruler, is in the 12th house, together with two other planets, making Virgo a central focus of the chart. Energetically, Venus is not very strong, but the chart has strength thanks to the blessing of exalted Jupiter in the 10th house.

A key point in Kate's chart is to balance Virgo and Pisces, analytical thinking and compassionate feelings. Similarly, to balance the sensitive feeling qualities of Venus with the practical rational perceptions of Virgo. In a balanced moment, Venus in Virgo displays admirable control and discrimination of our desires, but, when out of balance, it can become overburdened with self-doubts. Virgo can have a tendency to think too much, which can bring unhappiness with oneself. Virgo can even become overly critical of others. To judge oneself or others is dangerous as we can develop a habit of meanness of thought – I know this from personal experience of my own Virgo. We shouldn't be blind, but we should not dwell on the negative. Looking at positive qualities encourages them in ourselves and in others.

Yogananda said: "One who mentally dissects and analyzes the botanical properties of a flower misses a full appreciation of its beauty. But one who focuses on how beautiful that flower is, allowing one's intuitive feeling to respond to its pure essence, enjoys fully its loveliness."

Kate's chart

As Drupada said, Virgo is a perfectionist with great analytical powers, dividing things into small pieces to better learn and understand. Paying attention to details is important to become skillful, but it can also lead to being overly critical if we lose sight of the bigger picture, the uniting principle of love. The positive expression of Venus and Virgo in this chart can be found by realizing that Virgo likes to learn and understand, to find wisdom, while the highest quality of Venus is devotion – we can unite both and have devotion for wisdom.

Virgo has an enquiring attitude, asking a lot of questions to understand, but complete perception needs the insight of Pisces, and of water signs in general. The receptive qualities of the water element are potentially strong in this chart, mainly because Jupiter is in Cancer, but also, to a degree, because Ketu is in Pisces. In fact, Kate is kind and generous, watery qualities. It is necessary for everybody who is not a spiritual master, however, to go through a process of clarification of our feelings and intellect, so that our emotions do not cloud our mind, and our intellect does not neglect insight.

Although the ascendant is in an air sign, all the planets are in earth, water and fire signs. Earth is influential, because of the focus on Virgo and the fact that Moon is in an earth sign; this shows she is practical. Water is also quite apparent with Jupiter in the 10th house. Her kindness and friendliness have distinctive Cancer qualities.

It is interesting that Kate, who studies astrology, has often felt closer to the earth element than to water, while to me water is quite visible in her. I think this difference can be partly explained by the fact that her earthy perception comes from the inner 4th house, in an earth sign, while my outer point of view starts from the publicly visible 10th house, in a water sign.

Earth is the element that can give us stability, endurance, and practical skills for concrete goals and activities, but it is also the most solid element, so it can feel heavy and unyielding. The soul knows its own true nature is freedom, while on the material plane everything requires effort; we cannot achieve success without one-pointed concentration, will and energy. Life on the earth plane can be difficult, but it is also an opportunity to develop great strength of will. We all need the steadfastness of the earth element and we can develop it by realizing practical projects.

With the earth element we also need to be careful to not become bogged down by excessive focus on outer forms, whether actual material forms, or more subtle but still limiting forms like thought patterns.

For Kate, learning about the earth element has meant finding the steadfastness to carry out her work, but also gradually letting go of expectations, mostly of herself but also of others. Earth is tied to karma yoga, action without desire for the results.

Recently she has found it easier to become receptive, and she feels more comfortable with the spiritual work in the watery 10th house. Shunning the spotlight as a true 12th house kid, she always thought her contribution would be in the background. However, I believe Yogananda has pushed her in the forefront because of her great teaching skills; she even appeared on TV to discuss spirituality. Kriyananda similarly said that in the Ananda communities he never made project leaders those who wanted to lead, but rather those who had the capacity to serve.

Having Rahu in Virgo, opposite a water sign, signifies that our direction of growth is to develop discrimination, although without balance we can swing from excessive analysis to oversensitivity. In that case we will have a wrong mixture of water and earth: mud. Mud is neither stable like solid earth, nor clear and refreshing as pure water. To achieve balance of water and earth we need calmness. Calmness makes water intuitive and earth steadfast and determined.

Rahu in Virgo is potentially a contrary influence, which creates restlessness instead of calmness. Rahu likes to be active and creative, which is good for service, however it can make us too open and sensitive to worldly influences. Clear receptivity needs calmness of mind. We need to channel Rahu's energy and interest in practical activities, or it will go out of control.

At the same time, yoga techniques to calm and focus the mind are helpful – especially the Hong-Sau technique. Our breath and our mind are connected, and this meditation technique focuses

Kate's chart

and relaxes them both. It is explained in the Ananda worldwide website and freely available for anyone to learn – you don't know what you are missing! Rahu and Ketu are associated with breathing and the flow of energy in the spine. Hong-Sau gradually calms down our breathing; in turn this releases us from the compulsive control of the lunar nodes.

Virgo is the 6th sign of the natural zodiac, so it has similar qualities to the 6th house, which is more focused on personal effort. By contrast the 12th house, opposite, is a receptive house where we learn to receive inspiration and divine grace. Kate's Moon is in Capricorn, a sign of Saturn, which, similarly to Virgo, can be focused on practical efforts, as Capricorn is the active earth sign. Capricorn, Virgo and the 6th house are great for disciplined effort, and they sustain Kate's spiritual work, however these signs can make us neglect our innate happiness. In the 12th house, instead, we transcend our ego. This means we also have to transcend our personal effort and work – we need to do our best and let it go, leaving the results to divine will.

Reading her chart, Drupada said that if we focus too much on discipline and on the energy of Saturn and Virgo, it will not harmonize too well with Rahu. Rahu is especially influential because it is with Venus, the ascendant ruler. Rahu intensely dislikes boredom and discipline, so if we find that our efforts in work, meditation and service leave us dissatisfied, it would be helpful to realize that being a yogi is not all about hard work. Being a yogi is an adventure in finding divine bliss just behind our consciousness. The very same actions, done with different inner consciousness, can draw the good side of Rahu. Bliss and happiness are not just something we are supposed to find some day, in the future, but rather something that we gradually become aware of, and realize that it is increasingly real and present.

Because Rahu likes activity, some good ways to channel it are hatha yoga, mantra recitation, ceremonies, and even martial arts, like tai chi. Yogananda, in his school for children in India, was teaching yoga but also jujitsu and other martial arts. All these activities keep our mind busy, leaving less time for overly critical questioning.

Chapter Nineteen

Similar considerations on excessive intellectual focus are valid for Mercury with Sun in Leo. Because they are only two degrees apart, Mercury is combust and receives a lot of energy. This gives Kate a bright intellect, but can also lead to burning out.

Leo is the 11th house of community, and it is strong because of the Sun. Together with the 12th house and Jupiter, it indicates Kate's social involvement, especially with spiritual communities. The Sun also indicates visibility, as many people have benefited from her work. Her social work and visibility are in harmony with Libra, but not immediately with the 12th house, a house of seclusion which does not feel entirely comfortable with visibility. However, Kate also organizes yoga retreats, a combination of seclusion and social involvement that would cause less internal conflict with the 12th house.

The Sun is dominant in own sign, making Saturn not too happy in Leo, a rather personal sign. The planet of detachment in a strong fiery sign receives energy from the Sun, but it is less impersonal. When fire is not calm we can be irritable, harsh and impatient, but if we are calm then Saturn in Leo represents discrimination in using our energy. The wisdom of Saturn, a positive planet for Libra ascendants as it rules the benefic 5th house, is also good to prevent any Leo pride, in fact Kate is rather humble. However, if Saturn contracts too much with skepticism and perfectionism, it will constrict Sun's vitality and confidence.

To summarize Kate's chart, Libra is the active air sign, social and caring for others; Rahu with Venus in the 12th house indicates spiritual service; the three planets in the 11th house indicate social involvement in the community; the 10th house, with exalted Jupiter, is spiritual public action and karma yoga, while Cancer is the sign of personal caring for others, like a mother; Jupiter rules the 3rd house of motivation and the 6th house of service; the Moon in Capricorn is strong for practical projects; Mars rules the 7th house of relationships and is in the 12th house, indicating spiritual relationships; Mercury rules two houses of

Kate's chart

spirituality, the 9th and 12th, and is in the 11th of community; the 12th is the house of renunciation, which is normally associated with seclusion and isolation, however it is also similar to the sign of Pisces, so its true and complete meaning is transcending of the ego and receptivity to higher realities. All planets and signs combined clearly indicate Kate's spiritual involvement and benefic work in the world.

A similar interpretation can be read from the Moon. Taking the Moon as the new ascendant, all other planets are in the 7th house of relationships, 8th of transformation, and 9th of spirituality, except Ketu in the 3rd house. Reading my chart from the Sun I also have Ketu in the 3rd and Rahu in the 9th. The 3rd house is personal motivation, energy and will, while the 9th is divine grace. With the lunar nodes in these houses, we need to develop personal will, and attunement to divine will, personal effort and receptivity to divine grace. When Ketu is in the 3rd house we tend to rely more on personal will, so we need to focus especially on receptivity. If the lunar nodes were reversed we would have to focus more on expressing motivation and energy.

When I find myself relying too much on my own will, I like to remember the teachings of Jesus, that we are all children of God and we'll be taken care of.

Chapter Twenty

Shifu's chart

In Shifu's chart the strongest planets are exalted Mercury in Virgo, and Sun in Leo – earth and fire. We have seen before how neither Mars nor Venus are immediately at ease in Virgo, but here the strength of Mercury helps them to become more so. Sun, Mercury, Gemini and Virgo indicate a bright intellect with energy to realize practical projects. Because Mercury is in the 4th house and retrograde, however, Shifu is also comfortable with introspection.

The 7th house ruler is Jupiter, which is in the 12th house. For a person that is not too spiritual this could mean a difficulty in finding or keeping a partner, but for a yogi it indicates a spiritual partner, somebody who has some 12th house energy – in fact, Kate has an influential 12th house.

The 7th house ruler of Kate's chart is Mars, and it is in her 12th house as well, indicating her partner has Mars energy. Mars, mixed with Virgo and the 12th house, is assertive but not aggressive. The 7th house from her Moon has exalted Jupiter, suggesting a kind and spiritual partner.

Often friends or couples have a few planets in the same sign in both of their charts; good relationships have some common energy for ease of understanding, but also some differences to keep it interesting. Kate and Shifu have three planets in the same sign: Sun, Mars and Venus. Both also have Mercury retrograde and an air ascendant with its ruler in Virgo.

Shifu's ascendant is Gemini, so Venus rules the 12th house as well as the 5th house of intelligence, creativity and teaching. Mars rules the 6th house of service and the 11th house of community. Both Mars and Venus are with the ascendant ruler, making their meanings influential. This planetary combination in Virgo

Shifu's chart

describes social and spiritual involvement in helping others, just like in Kate's chart. The same considerations regarding the balance of Virgo and Pisces are also valid for Shifu, but with a subtle difference because Virgo here is the 4th house, and it is strong due to Mercury, while for Kate Virgo is the 12th house.

Mo	Ke	Ju	
			Sa
			Su
		Ra	Me Ve Ma

Shifu's chart. The ascendant is strong: its ruler is exalted in Virgo. The Sun in all charts indicates some of the same characteristics of the ascendant, like vitality and confidence, and it is strong in its own sign.

The 4th house is our internal state of mind and inner happiness, and in the natural zodiac it is Cancer. In this chart Saturn is in Cancer. Saturn is a fundamentally positive planet for Gemini ascendants because it rules the 9th house of spirituality, but being Saturn it can always bring some difficult karmic lessons. Cancer is the sign of mother and emotional well-being, and it is the most personal sign of the zodiac, while Saturn is the most impersonal planet. This can mean that, similarly to Saturn in Leo, Saturn in Cancer is less detached. In Leo, Saturn can become frustrated trying to control Leo's fiery expressions of energy. In Cancer, Saturn can weigh down our emotions by materializing in our life some unhappy circumstances, from past karma.

When this happens we might try to distance ourselves from our emotions, but that is not necessarily detachment. It can be a first step, but true detachment is selfless, liberating and compassionate, and to have it we need to strive for Truth. With this firm intention we can find a balance between personal and impersonal – both are expressions of wisdom.

On the other hand, Saturn in a water sign can be softer and kinder, while Moon is in Pisces, giving an inclination to compassion that balances Virgo and Saturn. Moon is in the 10th house, a strong position. In fact, Shifu is both confident and kind. His strength and vitality are especially obvious with the Sun in Leo. Leo is the 3rd house of motivated energy, so it can indicate martial arts – he is an expert karate teacher. I have practiced karate myself, and in my limited experience too many martial arts practitioners don't have a great sense of humour, but Shifu does and we both love *Kung Fu Panda*. Kindness of heart is shown by Moon and a bit by Venus, which is debilitated but drawing some strength from being in the 4th house with exalted Mercury. It is also indicated by Jupiter in Taurus, the ruler of the 7th house in a gentle and sociable sign. Shifu is also a confident communicator as his 3rd house would suggest.

Rahu and Ketu are in the 5th and 11th, linking again teaching and community, by house. By sign they indicate a focus on balancing Aries and Libra, spontaneous expression of energy and internal deliberation, independence and sensitivity to others. The 11th house is social, but it is also goal-oriented; in Aries, Ketu can indicate a habit of focus on our own goals. Rahu is our direction of growth, and in the 5th in Libra it shows that, by focusing on teaching and taking into account other people's feelings and opinions, we can expand our sense of self and increase our happiness.

Mars and Venus rule the two signs occupied by the nodes and they are both in Virgo, so to balance Rahu and Ketu we need to watch our response to Virgo's energy. Venus in Virgo can think too much, something to which any Gemini ascendant is especially susceptible. Similarly, Mars in Virgo can become hesitant.

Libra wants inner harmony with itself and with others, and

harmony needs receptivity; from that strong center of inner guidance we can be unhesitant in action, like Aries. Aries wants to take the initiative with or without guidance, while Libra can become too anxious to act. The tendency of Libra to be hesitant can be worsened by Virgo's influence on Venus and Mars, but exalted Mercury gives strength to both planets, so Virgo's influence will be subtle.

If we respond to Virgo by being too rational, critical and unsympathetic, it can worsen the possible tendency of Libra to withdraw from emotional involvement. Libra is an air sign so it can become too detached. Virgo's tendency to question excessive ego-involvement is a positive trait, but can be taken too far if we forget the compassion of Pisces, its opposite and complementary sign.

Virgo is a perfectionist, but as Asha said, we cannot perfect the ego, we need to transcend it. Rahu is driven and ambitious, so in Libra it seeks perfect harmony. This search, under the influence of Virgo, can become an exercise in futility, as perfectionism itself prevents us from finding harmony. A sliver of sincere devotion and receptivity can draw us closer to God than lifetimes of worrying over perfection.

When a chart points to a lesson we need to learn, it might be easy as yogis to catch obvious lapses in our response to the stars, or maybe believe it is safe now to forget about it – I've worked on it, it's gone now! But that lesson becomes progressively more subtle to see, and it remains valid until we completely dissolve that karma. Virgo should not take this comment as an invitation to worry unnecessarily about perfection.

We can see here a difference between Kate's chart and Shifu's. Both have an influential Virgo and Sun in Leo, however Kate's Leo is with Saturn while Shifu's is unaffected. Sun is strong in both cases, but since Saturn is not Sun's best friend, Shifu's Sun is stronger. Another difference is that the ascendant ruler of Shifu is exalted while Kate's is not strong in Virgo. Both the Sun and

Chapter Twenty

the ascendant ruler indicate confidence, so for Shifu self-doubt is not going to be a big problem, although it can still be a subtle veil that separates us from God in our mind. On the other hand, Kate has a very strong Jupiter, a blessing from her kindness and generosity in her past and present life, that will take her out of any self-doubt she might have, increasingly so as she becomes more receptive to that blessing. A strong Jupiter is a great balance for an excessively critical Virgo.

The higher expression of Virgo is discrimination and a strong capacity for pratyahara, interiorization of the mind. By drawing energy and inspiration from Spirit in meditation, we have an inexhaustible amount of energy for any outward activity, especially needed for the social and spiritual work of Kate and Shifu.

Going back to Rahu in Shifu's chart, it is worth remembering, with a strong Sun, that Libra is the diplomatic sign, which takes into consideration the opinion of others. Even when a situation calls for strong assertiveness, with Rahu in Libra we should make a special effort to be genuinely considerate, at all times, of how others, especially those close to us, will respond to our actions – not only thinking about it, as Virgo would do, but also feeling their reaction in our heart.

Similarly, Virgo's power of discrimination always needs to be balanced with the compassion of Pisces. This is something good for everybody to remember, regardless of our nodes position: to be kind to each other. These words of Jyotish and Devi, spiritual directors of Ananda worldwide, are especially relevant to Virgo:

"The deep sense of connectedness to God and other people that we gain in meditation is a large part of what produces an attitude of unity. It's important to carry that uplifted peace and harmony into our work and service. Yogananda said that meditation should be active service and that service should be active meditation.

If we can approach our work with a deep inward consciousness, our outer and inner life will begin to meld together into a beautiful, harmonious flow. The particular area of our work is not nearly so important as the quality of consciousness with which we work. Make it fun, joyful, cooperative, and holy."

Chapter Twenty One

Navamsha

The charts of Kate and Shifu have a focal point in Virgo, a sign I relate to from personal experience. This is not only because we all feel the influence of each sign to some degree, but especially because I have Virgo ascendant in my navamsha. The chart we have used till now is called rashi, from the sanskrit word for sign; I also call it natal as it's prominent at birth. The navamsha chart is derived from the rashi chart, and gives us additional information with emphasis on the potential direction we could go.

After some time of yoga practice and meditation, we should note some changes in ourselves. As time goes by, these changes will become more pronounced, and will be described by the navamsha. The natal or rashi chart always conserves its validity, but becomes gradually integrated with the navamsha.

Nav means nine and amsha division: the navamsha is made by dividing each natal sign into nine parts. The first of these nine divisions is assigned to the sign of the same element with the active modality. For example, we take Leo and divide it into nine parts. Leo is a fire sign, so the first part will be the active fire sign, Aries. The other eight parts of Leo follow the normal zodiac progression, so the 2nd division will be Taurus and the 9th Sagittarius. The same is done for all signs, so the first division of Virgo will be Capricorn and the 9th Virgo.

Dividing a sign in this way allows for a more in depth look of the energy within a sign. A planet will fall into one of these nine divisions, each of 3 degrees 20 minutes, and it will be given a new placement in the zodiac; we then draw a chart with these new planetary positions, obtaining the navamsha.

For example, if Mars is in the 6th degree of natal Scorpio, it is in its 2nd division (which goes from 3 degrees 20 minutes to

6 degrees 40 minutes). The active water sign is Cancer, so the 2nd division of Scorpio will be Leo. In navamsha, then, Mars will be in Leo.

The navamsha can be read exactly as the natal chart, keeping in mind that it is a more subtle chart – the natal chart has already manifested, the navamsha is more of a potential. A common saying in astrology is that the natal chart is the tree and the navamsha is the fruit. The positive potential of the navamsha can be realized with our efforts, and probably will become more evident as we get older. Should the direction be not so positive, we can correct it by knowing it in advance. The navamsha never substitutes the natal chart but allows a better look at energy patterns which are less evident.

It is even possible to create additional charts by different rules, always fractioning each sign into a number of parts. The number of divisions normally relates to the meanings of a house – if we divide each sign into four parts we obtain a divisional chart that looks more in depth at the 4th house. The 9th house is the most benefic and spiritual, the house of divine grace; for this reason the navamsha is the most important of the divisional charts, and the only one I use.

When we divide a sign into nine parts, the 1st will be active and of the same element, the 5th will be fixed of the same element, and the 9th mutable of that element. For example, if we divide Leo the 1st division will be Aries, the 5th Leo and the 9th Sagittarius. Just the same, if we divide Aries the 1st will be Aries, the 5th Leo and the 9th Sagittarius. These three divisions represent a sort of sub-modality within a sign: they are the beginning, middle and end of each sign. We could call them sub-active, sub-fixed, and sub-mutable. In this sense the pattern of energy within each sign has a Brahma, Vishnu, Shiva progression of beginning, depth and dissolution. For example, if the Sun is in the 1st division of Leo in the natal chart, it will be in Aries in navamsha, so the Sun will be fixed in modality from Leo, with a sub-flavor of active energy from Aries. In other words, the Sun is more active than we would have thought only by looking at the natal chart.

When a planet is in either of these three divisions (the 1st, 5th or 9th), its natal sign and its navamsha sign will be of the same element. The position of the planet in the two charts will be in harmony.

The harmony is greater if the planet is in the same sign in both charts. This happens only when a planet is in the 1st division of active signs, the 5th division of fixed signs, and the 9th division of mutable signs – for example, if a planet is in the 5th division of Leo, or the 1st division of Aries.

When a planet is in the same sign in the natal and navamsha chart it is vargottama. Uttama means principal, and varga means division, so vargottama means the best division. A planet that is vargottama is strong. When reading a chart for the first time I look mostly at the natal chart, but I give a quick look at the navamsha to see if any planet is vargottama, and also to see the general strength of each planet. If a planet is exalted in natal chart but debilitated in navamsha then it is still strong, but not as much. Vice versa, if a planet is weak in natal chart but strong in navamsha then it is not as weak.

An example of vargottama is Mars in the chart of Lahiri Mahasaya: it is exalted and vargottama, it is in the 4th house in the natal chart and in the 10th house in navamsha, it is an extremely strong Mars. Not surprising, considering that he reintroduced Kriya yoga to the world – a massive undertaking.

Another example is Adelle: both her Mars and exalted Sun are vargottama. In her chart this is useful to understand the strength of Mars, as Mars and Venus are neutral to each other by planetary friendship, so Taurus is sort of medium strength for Mars. We can see in the natal chart that Mars is influential because it is on the ascendant, but looking at the navamsha we also understand it has strength because it becomes vargottama. Her natal Sun is in the 12th house so it's hidden from view; in navamsha it goes onto the ascendant and its strength becomes very visible. Several people have told her that, when they got to know her better, they noticed she had more active energy than they thought she did when they first met her.

For a more detailed example lets take my navamsha. The ascendant is Virgo, intellectual and practical, and Mercury

Chapter Twenty One

is in Gemini in the 10th house, a strong placement. Mercury receives strength from the Sun in natal chart, and the navamsha certainly confirms its strength. My navamsha also helps explain my involvement in academia, as in the natal chart fire is stronger than air, while in navamsha the air element is more evident. Air is the academic element as it represents knowledge and intellectual activities.

The navamsha becomes more active with time, and certainly the strength of Gemini in navamsha has two positive effects which have become more evident recently: it strengthens my natal Gemini and Moon, and also Jupiter.

In fact, the navamsha and natal charts are linked, so the energy of a planet or sign in a chart varies following the influence of the other chart. The increase in energy of Mercury in navamsha, both by house and by sign, is transferred to Mercury in the natal chart, and indirectly to natal Gemini. Additionally, the strength of

			Me Ju
Ke			
Mo			
Ve			
	Su Ma		Sa Ra

Kashiraja's navamsha chart. The ascendant has two difficult planets in it, but it has strength from Mercury in its own sign in the 10th house.

Gemini in navamsha supports Gemini in the natal chart. Simply superimposing the navamsha chart onto the natal chart lets us directly see how corresponding signs link their energy. Jupiter and Mercury in navamsha, then, support the natal Moon, and help to draw out the best side of natal Ketu.

One thing that is immediately noticeable in my navamsha is Rahu and Saturn in Virgo. These two planets generally are the most challenging, and together they are often up to no good, because it is difficult to have a positive response to both of them united. It is difficult but not impossible, and with yoga and divine grace it can certainly be done. Saturn is practical and Rahu involves us in the world, so together they show some practical work to be done, especially in earthy Virgo. An obvious meaning is selfless service.

Considering that in my natal chart I have an influential Ketu with Moon, the fact that Rahu is on the ascendant in navamsha is an opportunity for balance. Not so good for balance is Saturn, which is too prominent in natal chart; the fact that it is on the ascendant in navamsha is not a cause for rejoicing. However, there it rules the benefic 5th house so it indicates Saturn becoming more positive. This potentiality will happen only if we make an effort to change our response to its energy. All the comments I made for Virgo in the charts of Kate and Shifu apply to me as well, summed up by the words of Yogananda: "....balance reason with empathy, understanding that every individual life is difficult, complex, and as deserving of sympathy as our own."

Rahu is our direction of growth, and in Virgo it means putting an emphasis on focus. Pisces can be very open, which is great to become more compassionate and receptive to higher insights, but receptivity also needs the one-pointed focus of Virgo, to concentrate on what we are trying to receive. Without focus Pisces can become confused, too open to influences which are not entirely positive – in that case Virgo can help by giving clarity of perception and discrimination. A practical way to increase Virgo's energy would be to practice japa, the repetition of God's name or other mantras, and also meditation and hatha yoga. When we are concentrated on some positive task our mind does not have energy to focus on negative things. This is an especially good response to Saturn, planet of concentration, and to Virgo, the sign of focused and calm attention; then Saturn can help Rahu and Virgo focus, otherwise Rahu has a tendency to be restless.

By contrast, Yogananda also had Rahu and Saturn together on the navamsha ascendant, but in watery Cancer; he was very devotional and a clear channel for Divine Mother.

Something to note for the nodes in my natal chart is that their flow of energy goes from Ketu in a Mercury sign to Rahu in a Jupiter sign, while the navamsha nodes go from Jupiter to Mercury. My intellectual energy of natal Gemini needs to be balanced with the upward aspirations of Sagittarius. Once I start to expand the mind with a deeper capacity for insight, first in natal Sagittarius and then in navamsha Pisces, I can return to Mercury's energy in navamsha Virgo.

Through this growth process, from Mercury to Jupiter and back to Mercury, I can achieve focus and critical thinking without getting lost into excessive reliance on the intellect alone. Without the Jupiter's inspiration, moving directly from Gemini to Virgo would not be a good idea, as my mind would remain overly critical and rational – it would be pure Mercury with no Jupiter.

Intellectual questioning is good, but it can be overdone and lead to negative doubts and skepticism, especially with my natal Jupiter in Capricorn. Excessive skepticism can make us diffident even of genuine happiness and joy. If balanced with Jupiter's energy, though, Virgo symbolizes purity of mind, focus on discipleship, and perfection in the practice of spiritual teachings.

After looking at the navamsha ascendant, we should probably continue with the stronger planets in the natal chart – apart from Saturn, these would be Sun and Mars. These friendly fiery planets are together in navamsha, in Scorpio; a profound sign for a yogi. Natal Mars is in Aquarius, a sign of knowledge which can be both spiritual but also scientific, while Scorpio is more interested in research of subtle subjects, like yoga and astrology. I noted earlier how my natal Sun needed to learn to be more receptive and sensitive, and now it is in a water sign, an opportunity for growth. In Aries, Sun is projecting strength and energy, while

Navamsha

in Scorpio it looks within with intensity. In navamsha, Scorpio is also the 3rd house of writing, Mars rules the 8th and Sun the 12th – a good combination to write about spiritual yogic astrology.

The Moon also expands its view as it goes from natal Gemini to navamsha Aquarius; both are air signs but Aquarius is more impersonal and searching for universal knowledge. When a planet moves from one natal sign to a different navamsha sign we can interpret it as a direction of growth, without implying a negative connotation on the original planetary placement. In this case it shows a shift of interest from intellectuality to spiritual wisdom.

Venus becomes more impersonal as well, moving from Taurus to a sign of Saturn. In Taurus, Venus can be attracted to material beauty per se; with an infusion of Saturn and Capricorn, Venus is more detached and wants to love Spirit through form, not form itself.

Overall, the house that seems to improve the most is the 10th. In natal chart it is most afflicted: from the ascendant it is blocked by Saturn; from the Moon its ruler is debilitated Jupiter; from the Sun it is occupied by debilitated Jupiter. In navamsha, instead, from the ascendant it has Mercury in own sign; from the Moon it has Mars in own sign; from the Sun its ruler is Sun, which is in a strong friendly sign.

Another house that shows progress is the 5th: in the natal chart its ruler is weak and it is only occupied by Rahu. Rahu and Ketu are not material planets, so Rahu is more of an indication of the need to develop the 5th house rather than an actual planetary presence. A physical planet in the 5th house would demonstrate a developed energy of some kind. In navamsha, however, Venus occupies the 5th house and its ruler is on the ascendant, indicating that this house is manifesting actual energy.

Between reading the natal chart, the navamsha chart, and even superimposing the two, we suddenly get a lot more information. I usually pay more attention to the navamsha only in subsequent readings. However, if someone is a little older and they have made efforts to improve themselves then the navamsha can be quite relevant.

Chapter Twenty Two

Relative planetary placements

A simple method to assess the degree of harmony between planetary positions in the natal and navamsha charts is to count the number of signs that divides them. Planets which are 5 or 9 signs apart are in harmony, as their signs will have the same element – for example Jupiter in natal Aries and in Leo in navamsha. When we count signs from a planet, we are taking it as a specific point of view, so, for example, planets in the 5th sign from it are in the benefic 5th house for that planet. We can count signs for the same planet in natal and navamsha chart, or even for the same planet in the natal charts of two people, if we want to analyze their compatibility as friends or as a couple. We can also count signs to look at the relationship between two different planets, say Sun and Jupiter in a single natal chart.

When comparing the charts of a couple, we can also look at the compatibility of the natal chart of one with the navamsha of the other, to see if the future potential of one navamsha is agreeable with the present of the other. We can even compare the two navamshas to see if the couple is moving in a similar direction. We shouldn't take these comparisons as too restrictive, but they can be a useful indication; what is important is to understand with clarity and wisdom the underlying relationship between planets, rather than simply counting signs.

An example of a 5-9 placement is the Moon of Kriyananda: it is in Leo in natal chart and in Aries in navamsha. In both cases it is in a fire sign in the 3rd house of motivated energy, communication and writing, and he certainly has a lot of energy, especially in those areas.

Apart from 5-9, another obviously harmonious relationship is 1-1 as it is vargottama, same sign, element and modality.

Relative planetary placements

If the signs have same modality but different element, there is some common ground but also some differences, it is a dynamic connection and can be energetic and positive. This is called 4-10. An example is Cancer and Aries: both are active, one is sensitive while the other fiery and independent, together they have the possibility to find a balance of different qualities. Of course there is also the potential for some great misunderstanding, as Aries can be too blunt and Cancer overly sensitive. A 4-10 is not as easy as 5-9, but there is a common ground as both signs enjoy dynamic activity. A similar example is Taurus and Leo, fixed earth and fixed fire: Taurus is gentle but can be insecure, while Leo is confident but can be insensitive. They are both fixed so they can be steadfast and perhaps a bit immovable and unyielding, but they can understand this trait in each other.

A special case of different element but same modality is that of opposite signs, 7-7: it is a complementary relationship and quite harmonious and fruitful. Opposite signs are always either air and fire or water and earth. As a broad categorization, air and fire like to project while water and earth are receptive. As a consequence a 7-7 placement has a degree of harmony which is slightly higher than 4-10. Both have different element and same modality, but 7-7 has the easier pairing for the elements.

All the other placements have different modality and element so they can be more difficult.

A 3-11 placement is potentially harmonious but it requires some work. An example is Aries and Gemini: Aries likes to act, Gemini likes to think, however both like movement and change, so they can develop an understanding even though they have different element and modality. Another example is Scorpio and Capricorn: one is rather personal and intense, the other practical and impersonal. However, Scorpio can learn some discipline from Capricorn, and Capricorn can moderate its skepticism, and learn to intuitively feel the depths of immaterial consciousness of Scorpio. Signs which are 3 or 11 counts apart, just like opposite signs, are always either air and fire or water and earth. Their element and modality are different, but the pairing for the elements is easier.

The last two planetary relationships, 2-12 and 6-8, are the most

Chapter Twenty Two

difficult planetary placements. They have different element and modality, and the element pairing is not easy. The 6-8 is more difficult than the 2-12 because the 6th, 8th and 12th houses are considered the most challenging houses: the 2-12 has one difficult house, while the 6-8 has two.

An example of 2-12 is Pisces and Aries, one representing expansive openness and compassion, the other independent thinking and initiative. We can make them work together beautifully but not before some dedicated communication. Aries especially needs to do something uncharacteristic and develop sensitivity and understanding for something outside itself. Pisces is probably going to have an easier time to adjust to Aries, because being a water sign it is open and not aggressive. Although, Pisces could be too sensitive then it may be hurt by blunt Aries. The 12th house is not an easy house for the ego, so a placement in the 12th is more challenging than one in the 2nd.

Another example of 2-12 is Taurus and Aries. My favorite image from Drupada's classes is when he compares Taurus to a water buffalo, happily basking in his own pond and rather unwilling to move – quite the opposite of Aries. The water buffalo might not be the cutest animal, but I find its philosophy is, and I wholeheartedly agree with it. I may have a strong Aries but my Venus is in Taurus so that is where you'll find my heart. The natural progression of the zodiac is from Aries to Taurus, so Aries can adapt to Taurus better as it can understand the need for sustaining energy after the beginning of a project. The opposite direction, from Taurus to Aries, is slightly more challenging – Taurus is not too fond of quick change and new beginnings!

It is certainly possible to make any planetary relationship work, however it is different if certain placements are in our chart, in which case we have no choice but to work on them, or if they are in the chart of someone else, then we do have a choice. If we find it difficult to relate to planets that are in very different signs to ours, we may have some troubles and misunderstandings with certain people – their charts will be challenging for us. In that case, we need to consider whether it is a good idea to spend a lot of time together, like entering a business relationship or getting married. It might be best to just be friends!

Overall, if between the charts of different people we have several planets in harmony, some difficulty in communication for a few planets is not a problem. But if several planets are in challenging positions, then the relationship might not be easy, in spite of some superficial or karmic attraction. One especially important point is the ascendant. For example, I and my wife have a 4-10 in the ascendant, and 1-1 and 5-9 for our ascendant rulers, so the 6-8 for our Moon positions is not a big deal, especially because we have good connections also through the navamsha. In fact, a 6-8 could mean that we help each other transform in a spiritual way, because the 8th house is the house of transformation.

However, in general 6-8 is the most obstructive planetary relationship. Signs 6 or 8 counts apart don't have a lot in common and they both need to go through a transformation to be able to communicate. An example would be Aries and Virgo. Virgo is a critical and practical thinker, so Aries feels weighed down by it; Virgo can be hesitant with self-doubts and does not know what to do with the willful energy of Aries. To compare it with the 3-11 of Aries and Gemini, Virgo is more critical than Gemini, so Mars is more uncomfortable with Virgo than with Gemini.

Pisces and Leo are another 6-8 placement and they also are quite different. Leo is assertive but may be too proud and insensitive, Pisces is sensitive and intuitive but may be too easily swayed and lack confidence. It is worth the challenge to bring a 6-8 together: with a balance of Leo and Pisces, we would be confident, strong, sensitive and intuitive.

To summarize, when planets are in signs with the same element or modality, they are more likely to get along; the 3-11, 2-12 and 6-8 placements have neither element nor modality in common and are progressively more difficult, in that order.

Counting signs can be useful but we should not rely on it exclusively or too rigidly. For example, my natal and navamsha placements for the Sun are in a 6-8. There might be some challenge in harnessing the fiery energy of Sun with self-control, first in natal Aries and then in navamsha Scorpio. However, both are signs of Mars, a friend of the Sun. Aries is my natal 9th house of

Chapter Twenty Two

spirituality, while Scorpio is the 3rd house of motivated energy in navamsha. The link between the 9th and 3rd houses, with Scorpio's energy, is good for studying and practising spiritual subjects, like yogic astrology. With a 6-8 the Sun moves into the 8th house from its natal position – a spiritual transformation.

Chapter Twenty Three

Chart of Paramhansa Yogananda

Yogananda had Leo ascendant and certainly fulfilled the highest aspect of Leo, shining light around him, and helping others to remember their true soul nature. The Moon on his ascendant represents the divine balance of fiery willpower and softer watery kindness, something that was quite evident in his life. In navamsha the ascendant is Cancer, confirming our interpretation. The Moon is sociable and he was often surrounded by friends. In the rashi chart it also rules the 12th house of spirituality and renunciation, in fact he was a Swami. Fire and water are his strongest elements and he possessed their perfected traits: energy, enthusiasm, compassion, and intuition.

The ascendant ruler in the natal chart is in Sagittarius, a friendly sign to the Sun, and is together with Mercury in the benefic 5th house of teaching and counselling: he had a bright intellect and he was a joyful and enthusiastic teacher. While in USA he went on a wide tour of public lectures, attended by thousands of people at a time: Leo can be charming.

One of Yogananda's teachings is about the power of magnetism: positive magnetism will attract good and spiritual things as well as necessary material things, while negative magnetism will attract difficulties. Most importantly, he stressed that we can change our magnetism every moment by the application of one-pointed willpower. At other times he impressed the importance of attunement and receptivity to God and guru. These are examples of the integration of willful Leo and receptive Moon.

Yogananda as a teacher personified Venus, the teacher of those who are still enmeshed in desires, but also Jupiter, the teacher of advanced yogis. By contrast, Sri Yukteswar's teaching methods were more acceptable to advanced souls, that is why he sent

Chapter Twenty Three

Yogananda on a spiritual mission to the West, which he could better accomplish thanks to his evident kindness.

Yogananda's diplomatic ways and uncompromising principles are a perfect blend of Aries and Libra, his lunar nodes signs: their rulers have a 5-9 relationship. Rahu is in Aries, in the 9th house, in fact he was resourceful and innovative in his teaching methods. He was the first yogi to come and live in USA, back when yoga was not well known at all, and he used modern tools like newspaper advertisements, conferences and worldwide publication of books. He also put together the Energization Exercises, a 10 minutes physical routine which energizes the body, befitting Aries and Rahu who both like activity.

Observing the natal and navamsha nodes we can see a flow throughout his life, moving from natal Ketu to natal Rahu and then from navamsha Ketu to navamsha Rahu. In the natal chart, Ketu is in the 3rd house in Libra. Even though he came liberated, he lived the life of a disciple to set an example for us all, which he recorded in his autobiography. The 3rd house is about personal will, and in Libra it shows how to deepen our inner harmony, through meditation and finding a guru. This is the first part of his life.

Later he goes to USA to begin his mission in the West, signified by Rahu in Aries, a new beginning. This work took a lot of strength, determined effort and hard work, dealing with many practical issues, like buying land and buildings for the yoga centers, and paying bills; this is indicated by Ketu in earthy Capricorn in navamsha. He also created the most beautiful garden at Lake Shrine, a small lake surrounded by flowers, close to the ocean on Sunset Boulevard in Los Angeles, a place that even today is inspiring thanks to his loving presence.

In the final part of his life he spent more time with his closest disciples, or in seclusion, writing books – or better, dictating them – during retreats in the Californian desert. This is shown by Rahu and Saturn in Cancer, two planets which like to be busy with practical work, but are within the sign of Cancer. Capricorn is the active earth sign, very appropriate for building a home, but Cancer is now enjoying the comfort of that home, directing the practical energy of Rahu and Capricorn in a direction closer to the water element: receiving inspiration for writing, and sharing that insight with a closer family of disciples.

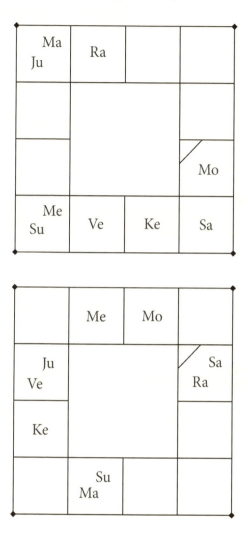

Yogananda's chart. The ascendant for the rashi chart (top) is strong because the Sun is in the benefic 5th house in friendly Sagittarius. Sagittarius receives strength from its ruler in Pisces. In navamsha, the ascendant ruler is exalted and Venus is in the sign of a friend together with the 9th house ruler.

Chapter Twenty Three

Drupada makes an interesting comment about Yogananda's 8th house, in both rashi and navamsha chart. Yogananda said he used to heal people, but then they would go back to their old ways, so he rather wanted to help them change. The 6th house is the house of healing, but there is no planet there in either chart. Instead, in the rashi chart the 8th house of transformation is strong because of Jupiter and Mars, which rule the 5th, 8th and 9th houses: teaching spiritual transformation. Additionally, Venus and Jupiter, the teacher planets, are in a 5-9 placement in natal chart and together in the 8th house in navamsha. Another similar indication is that Mars and Sun are in Scorpio in navamsha, making it strong; Scorpio is the 8th sign of the natural zodiac, which is similar to the 8th house.

Yogananda gives us a beautiful message through his navamsha ascendant, Cancer. Cancer is a sign that loves to be comfortable at home, not normally associated with hard work. Yogananda came liberated: he had the choice to remain in India, walking by the Ganges drunk with God, free of any earthly responsibilities. However, he came to USA, dealing with all sorts of material difficulties, to helps us find happiness. These are some verses from one of his poems, *God's Boatman*:

I want to ply my boat, many times,
Across the gulf after death,
And return to earth's shores
From my home in space.
I want to load my boat
With all those waiting, thirsty ones
Who have been left behind,
That I may carry them to the opalescent pool
Of iridescent joy,
there where my Father distributes
His all-desire-quenching, liquid peace.
Oh! I will come back again and again!
Crossing a million crags of suffering,
With bleeding feet, I will come,
If need be, a trillion times,

Chart of Paramhansa Yogananda

As long as I know that
One stray brother is left behind.

That dedication, manifested in the material plane, is represented by Rahu and Saturn on the ascendant in navamsha. His mission was ultimately successful, as his teachings strengthened the growing spiritual awareness of many people, and to this day are a lasting influence on yoga practitioners worldwide, but especially in Los Angeles and USA.

His success is indicated by the ascendant ruler in navamsha, exalted Moon in the 11th house of community. It was an important theme to Yogananda which had influential consequences. Once, during a public speech, he vehemently described the need for people to live in spiritual communities, and how in future this would be the standard way of living. He was only able to establish a monastery during his lifetime but his work was continued by Swami Kriyananda, who founded several Ananda communities throughout the world.

Chapter Twenty Four

Chart of Swami Kriyananda

Kriyananda has dedicated his life to continuing the work of Yogananda, with whom he lived as a disciple for the last few years of the master's life. Kriyananda has published a lot of books on spiritual subjects and their practical applications, and he has helped establish various Ananda communities dedicated to living the teachings of Yogananda. His subtle understanding of many subjects fits well with his Gemini ascendant. Mercury, the ascendant ruler, is in the 11th house in Aries, indicating the groundbreaking fiery energy required to start this spiritual and social work.

A notable influence is Rahu on the ascendant: Kriyananda has perfected his response to Rahu's energy, expressing its higher potential as selfless service. Both lunar nodes are very strong in Gemini and Sagittarius, and are vargottama – he has fiery enthusiasm and a perceptive mind. Gemini can be the most subtle sign of the zodiac: it is the mutable air sign, in the ether chakra which transcends the grosser elements. Gemini does need, however, calmness and interiorization. An overused Mercury can cause mental stress and even a nervous breakdown, but Kriyananda demonstrates the best response to Mercury's energy, through meditation and attunement to Spirit.

Rahu on the ascendant indicates selfless karma yoga; a similar meaning is given by Saturn, the 9th house ruler in the 6th house of service, in deep and metaphysical Scorpio. Saturn is in a sign of Mars, however, and Mars is the most difficult planet for Mercury ascendants. As a consequence, he has gone through some troubles in the past, especially since the 6th house is the house of health problems – of which he has had many. As his body grows older it is as if he is burning its physical vitality to continue fueling his work, not too concerned by physical pain because he has divine bliss.

Chart of Swami Kriyananda

Ve	Me	Su	Ra
Ju Ma			Mo
Ke	Sa		

Ma	Mo		Ra
Su			Sa
Ve			
Ke	Ju		Me

Kriyananda's chart. The ascendant ruler in the rashi chart (top) is in the 11th house, while the 11th house ruler is in the 9th house with benefic Jupiter. Venus, a friend of Mercury, is exalted. Mercury is exalted in navamsha, increasing its strength in the natal chart.

Mars rules the 6th house for a Gemini ascendant, and the 8th house for a Virgo ascendant, two houses which can be challenging; it rules no benefic house in either case so it can be a difficult planet, especially for Saturn who is not comfortable in Mars' signs.

Chapter Twenty Four

On the other hand, Mars is in the 9th house, the most benefic house. Mars and Saturn are each in the sign of the other, an exchange of energy that improves their communication. It is always possible, by controlling our response to the stars, to make any difficult planet work in a positive way, however mutual exchange of signs can certainly help two planets become more friendly to each other. For Gemini ascendants, Saturn rules the 8th house of transformation and the 9th house of spirituality, while Mars rules the 6th house of karma yoga and the 11th house of community: Kriyananda has certainly been able to bring their energies harmoniously together.

Saturn's job is often to bring obstacles, but in the 6th house of obstacles it also means having strength to overcome obstacles. In fact, he's been able time after time to defeat any obstacle. Saturn is in the 6th house in navamsha as well, where it rules the ascendant and the 12th house: renunciation, karma yoga, discipleship and adherence to Truth are all evident Saturn traits in Kriyananda. Saturn is in a water sign in both rashi and navamsha charts.

Also in a water sign is Venus, which is very strong in the natal chart because exalted in the 10th house of public work. Ruling the benefic 5th house of teaching and the spiritual 12th house, Venus indicates Kriyananda's compassionate effort to expand everybody's consciousness. He always presents his work as coming from Yogananda, not as a way to justify his personal authority, but with the intention of being a channel and putting his ego aside, until it disappears – a truly Piscean attitude of discipleship. This humbleness is also indicated by the ruler of the 9th house of guru in the 6th house of discipleship. His attunement is also evident in the fact that Kriyananda has Moon in Leo, the same placement of Yogananda's Moon, as if to say they are of one mind.

Venus loves art and Kriyananda has composed a lot of inspirational music. He says melodies come to him in his mind already formed, and he only makes some adjustment during revision. This is the capacity for profound intuition that we can all achieve, especially in watery signs like Pisces. Yogananda explains how to develop it: "The power and largeness of your inner receptivity determine how much, and how quickly, you can

Chart of Swami Kriyananda

grasp knowledge. By awakening the brain cells through meditative practices, you can increase your receptivity. The receptivity of the brain cells can become so great that you can quickly grasp whatever knowledge you need. The person of great receptivity quickly sees everything. In a single lifetime, you will be able to absorb within yourself everything you need to know."

Pisces is the 10th house in the rashi chart, and its ruler, Jupiter, is in Aquarius with Mars. The four houses ruled by Jupiter and Mars are, apart from the 10th, the 7th house of relationships, the 6th of service and the 11th of communities. These houses are combined in Aquarius, the 9th house. Aquarius is the fixed air sign, with an impersonal desire to acquire and share wisdom with others, a good sign for Jupiter who loves wisdom. Drupada notes how past adversities in the public work of Kriyananda are indicated by the difficult nature of Mars as the 6th house ruler, bringing obstacles to the 10th house ruler Jupiter. These obstacles were caused by opposition from others to his willful efforts in continuing Yogananda's work. Mars in Aquarius in 9th house represents fiery energy in sharing knowledge, something that was disagreeable to some.

Pisces and Aquarius were similarly evident in Yogananda, as his natal Jupiter and Mars were in Pisces, while in navamsha he had Jupiter and Venus in Aquarius. Yogananda was very devotional and compassionate but in later works his impersonal Aquarian energy is more evident, especially in his commentary to the Bhagavad Gita. Masters are always one with God and can express any divine quality they wish, but they put on a personality during an incarnation, probably for the benefit of their specific mission; maybe, also because every soul retains a memory of its unique individuality even when liberated.

Aquarius, as a sign of Saturn, represents the wisdom of detachment, and Kriyananda often mentions the importance of equanimity of mind to find inner freedom, the door to eternal bliss.

When he talks of his younger self, he sometimes mentions that he was a bit too intellectual; this can happen to Gemini as it is an air sign, while Rahu is airy in character and it can draw us too much out of our center. However, he got rid of this tendency

Chapter Twenty Four

when he became a disciple of Yogananda.

His ascendant ruler in natal chart is in Aries, which is a neutral sign to Mercury, so energetically it is not overly strong. However, he improved it over time and his efforts have come to fruition, as we can also see in his navamsha, where Mercury becomes exalted.

Of course his natal chart has other strengths, notably exalted Venus, but it remains an example of how we don't need an exalted ascendant ruler to have a strong natal chart. What matters is always our response to the energy of the planets. We all have the innate ability to draw strength through means outside the realm of the stars, by our attunement to God.

Chapter Twenty Five

Vimshottari dasha

The influence of the planets changes over time depending on many factors, some based on our choices, others controlled by their own natural flow, which can be described by certain astrological techniques. One such technique divides our life into time periods, each ruled by a planet which exerts a special influence during those years. These periods are called dashas. There are many different dasha systems, but the most commonly used is called vimshottari, meaning 120. The vimshottari dasha system assigns a fixed number of years to each of the nine planets for a total of 120 years: Ketu 7 years, Venus 20, Sun 6, Moon 10, Mars 7, Rahu 18, Jupiter 16, Saturn 19, Mercury 17. Astrology is an ancient science and the reason for these numbers is not publicly known.

Which dasha is the first is determined by the position of the Moon in the natal chart, though not relative to the signs we have used so far, but to the nakshatras, or lunar signs. For now, since we haven't looked at the nakshatras yet, suffice to say that the Moon will be within a lunar sign, and the ruler of this nakshatra will rule the first dasha.

How much that dasha lasts is proportional to how much progress the Moon has made in the lunar sign. For example, if the Moon's position in the natal chart is at 1/3 of a lunar sign ruled by the Sun, then we will start at 1/3 of the Sun dasha. Since the complete Sun dasha lasts 6 years, we will have 4 years left of it from the time of birth. During these years the Sun's energy will be emphasized in our life.

The next dasha follows in the same planetary order listed above, with its complete duration. In our example the next dasha would be Moon, lasting 10 years. In these 10 years the Moon would be more influential.

Chapter Twenty Five

The overall influence of a dasha ruler depends on its position in the chart. Generally speaking, if the planet is benefic or in a good placement its dasha will be easier than if the planet were in a difficult position in the chart.

Often when a dasha changes it is quite noticeable. For example, Adelle, from age 4 to 23, was in the dasha of Saturn which then changed to Mercury. Saturn is slow so it is oriented to tradition, it doesn't like quick change much. Mercury is quick and agile, and in her chart is with Rahu, both of which like change. When Adelle entered Mercury's dasha she went to live on her own for the first time and she started practising yoga and meditation. Mercury is in Pisces, the most open and receptive sign – it helped her become more open to new influences, which were positive thanks to the strong and favorable Jupiter.

Her new dasha strengthened Rahu indirectly, so in a way during Saturn's dasha Ketu and Saturn were more visible, while in the new dasha Rahu and Mercury become more influential. Ketu is in Virgo in her chart, an intellectual earthy sign, and Saturn is the planet of concentration: the two had a positive influence together, helping her focus towards graduation from university. However Saturn, and Ketu in Virgo, can be dry, so Mercury and Rahu brought balance by expanding the mind in Pisces. This is how Adelle described the transition between the two dashas: "I sincerely enjoyed to analyze and over analyze things, together with a friend, it was a hobby that we indulged in often. But now, those things don't interest me, I have a more practical approach. It's not that I stopped analyzing, but I don't go as crazy with it. Also, now, I do rely on my intuition more, though I did quite a bit earlier as well. This might be because I trust it more. In college it did get a bit dry at times, because I started to question the existence of God and tried to solely rely on science and psychology, which were somewhat helpful, but they weren't enough."

Each dasha lasts for several years. We can look more in depth at each period by dividing it into smaller sub-periods, also called 2nd level periods. To do so, we take each dasha and divide it using the same proportions assigned to the planets which we used in the 1st dasha level. For example, Ketu rules a dasha of 7 years, so

Vimshottari dasha

it has a fraction of the total 120 years equal to 7/120; Venus rules 20 years so it has a fraction of 20/120.

When dividing a dasha, the first sub-period will be of the same planet which rules the dasha, continuing with the others in the normal order. For example, to divide the Venus dasha of 20 years into 9 sub-periods, we assign the first sub-period to Venus with a fraction of 20/120. This makes it 20/120 times 20 years of Venus dasha, or about 3 years and 4 months. The next sub-period will be Sun, lasting 6/120 times 20 years, which is 1 year.

We can further divide each sub-period into sub-sub-periods (or 3rd level periods) following a similar rule, and even go on with the 4th and 5th levels, but the finer divisions are quite sensitive on having a precise birth time. We can usually look up to the 3rd level with enough confidence as they last a few months each, so they will just change by a few days if the birth time is wrong by a few minutes. The 4th and 5th levels are so short that if the birth time is not correct they might be completely off.

To continue with Adelle's chart (on page 94), she was born in a European country but immigrated to USA with her family in her Saturn-Venus-Rahu 3rd level period. This period lasted about five months. Saturn was ruling its dasha of 19 years, while Venus was ruling its sub-period of about 3 years. Within this time, Rahu had a special influence during the specific five months of its 3rd level period. Rahu likes change and one of its meanings is foreign countries. For Adelle it is in the 11th house of gains, with Jupiter, so we could expect a positive change. The 11th is also the house of community so it can indicate a change in community. Then we have to bring into the interpretation the meanings of Saturn and Venus: Saturn is not in the easiest sign in Scorpio, and it is in the 7th house of relationships. Certainly it wasn't easy for a young girl to leave her friends, and move to a new country where she had to learn a new language. However, Saturn also rules the benefic 9th house and Venus is a benefic planet, so the change was for the best as she moved to a country with much greater opportunities. Saturn rules the 10th house and Venus occupies it, so we could think that the move was also good for her future work and career.

151

Chapter Twenty Five

Years later, at the end of Saturn's dasha, in Saturn-Jupiter-Rahu, she found a job and her own flat. Again we see Rahu's influence for change, made favorable by Jupiter, whose expansive qualities temper the difficult side of Saturn and let it act more as the benefic 9th house ruler. Jupiter, Rahu and Saturn are also either in 1-1 or 5-9, harmonious placements.

She officially started working and moved out of her family's house at the very beginning of the new dasha, in Mercury-Mercury-Mercury. Mercury rules the benefic 5th house and also the 2nd, an artha house of supportive things, which in the general sense could include having the financial security of a job and the stability of her own home.

A few months later, she started practising yoga in an Ananda center in Mercury-Mercury-Venus. Venus is in Aquarius in the natal chart, emphasising her interest in acquiring knowledge, thanks to the energy of the new dasha of Mercury, in the 3rd level period of Venus. This doesn't mean we are all puppets controlled by the stars, as Adelle had to make the choice to actually use this energy in the way she did. The planets encouraged her in a certain way during specific periods, but her response to this influence determined what happened. Her actions were caused to some extent by her free will, and to some extent by the energetic habits she had created in the past, her past karma. Her karma came to fruition at specific times according to spiritual laws, which we can gleam at through astrology and intuition. In this case, Venus was an agent of good karma, a seed of interest in spiritual knowledge that sprouted at a favorable time, to which Adelle responded by watering it with fresh willpower and receptivity.

Continuing the theme of new and quick energy of Mercury's dasha, she met her future husband in Mercury-Mercury-Moon, then she got engaged in Mercury-Mercury-Mars: the Moon is in the 7th house of relationships and Mars is its ruler. In Mercury-Mercury-Rahu she quit her job and left the state for a while. Now she is in Mercury-Ketu, a good opportunity to balance the previous Rahu period. We have seen in her chart that normally Rahu's side is stronger, but eventually we need to balance the nodes. Ketu's sub-period might bring some feeling of lack of energy because it can bring our energy down, in contrast to Rahu who activates our energy. However, if we are able to attune ourselves to higher realities, Ketu brings insights down from higher levels of perception.

In the chart of Swami Kriyananda, Saturn rules the 8th and 9th houses in the natal chart, and the 1st and 12th houses in navamsha: spiritual transformation and renunciation. It also occupies the 6th house of karma yoga and discipleship in both charts. Saturn is especially influential for Kriyananda because it has a direct connection with his Moon. This connection is found through a special rule of astrology which says that Saturn sends its energy not only in the sign opposite, like every planet, but also in the 3rd and 10th signs counted from Saturn.

When a planet sends its energy to another sign it is called an aspect. Every planet aspects the sign opposite but Saturn also aspects the 3rd and 10th signs. Jupiter and Mars are the only two other planets with these special aspects: Jupiter aspects the 5th and 9th signs from it, which are of the same element of the sign it occupies; Mars aspects the 4th and 8th signs. These special aspects are not always of primary importance, but in the case of Kriyananda the Moon is in the 10th sign from Saturn in both natal and navamsha charts, indicating Saturn's special influence. The combination of Moon and Saturn is not always easy, but in this case it clearly indicates spirituality and renunciation.

Another spiritual planet in his chart is exalted Venus, which rules the 12th and 5th houses. Considering the influence of Saturn and Venus it is not surprising that Kriyananda met Yogananda and became his disciple in the Venus-Saturn period.

Venus and Saturn are in a 5-9 placement and are planetary friends. I think it was in Venus-Saturn-Rahu that he left his home and travelled coast to coast to find his guru, with whom he remained until Venus-Ketu, when Yogananda left his body. Ketu is in Kriyananda's 7th house and indicates his great ability to intuitively understand others, together with the insightful and strong Pisces which is occupied by exalted Venus. However, Ketu

Chapter Twenty Five

is a hermit yogi, complementary to Rahu which involves us in the world, so it can have a divisive influence. Perhaps here it also indicates a separation in body, though not in Spirit, from his guru.

It was probably in Venus-Mercury-Mercury that Kriyananda heard the public speech that Yogananda gave about spiritual communities: Mercury is in the 11th house of community in Aries, while benefic Venus is exalted in the 10th house. The thought remained impressed in his mind, leading years later to the foundation of Ananda Village in northern California, the first and largest of Ananda centers. I think the community started either in his Moon-Venus or Moon-Sun period. The Moon is in the 3rd house of motivated energy, in charming Leo, opposite the 9th house in Aquarius, which is occupied by Jupiter and Mars. Leo is a sign of leadership.

Officially, Ananda Village was founded a year later, in his Mars-Mars-Mercury. Mars rules the 11th house and Mercury occupies it. Mars is the planet of energy and it is in the 9th house of divine grace and guru, with Jupiter. At the transition between Moon and Mars dashas we find the energy and will of Swami Kriyananda, as well as the spiritual blessing of Yogananda, that made Ananda possible.

Eventually, other Ananda communities were formed worldwide, for example one in Gurgaon (India) in his Jupiter-Venus period. Probably this community took less work to get started, being directly under the influence of exalted Venus in the 10th house, and Jupiter in the 9th!

Anything is possible in any dasha, with divine grace and willpower, but it can be useful to be aware of the astrological weather forecast to plan accordingly.

Although the dashas of benefic planets should generally be easier, a lot depends on the position of the dasha ruler in the chart, what planets it is connected to, and most importantly our response to its influence. For example, the years of my Jupiter dasha were most difficult. Jupiter is a benefic planet in general, and in my chart especially as it rules the 5th house, however it is debilitated in the 6th, a challenging position. I was not able to respond to its energy in the right way, and in fact several times I was too open to negative influences. I did have a blessing though: I got to read the autobiography of Yogananda. That seed of spiritual influence remained in the back of my mind, and sprouted many years later during Saturn's dasha. Saturn is a difficult planet in my chart but it was during its dasha that I got my life back on track. I studied for my first physics degree in Italy, and in Saturn-Venus-Rahu I went to UK to continue my studies. Venus supported the positive side of Saturn and Rahu brought me abroad.

In Saturn-Venus-Saturn I moved to Cambridge to start my PhD. Saturn and Venus are friends and they are strong together in the 10th house. Now the 3rd level planet was Saturn, not Rahu, so the 10th house of public work became evident. In Europe a PhD position does not include any formal coursework, so it is a full time job (though it is the least paid, most qualified job in the world).

Another technique we can use to evaluate a dasha is to take the dasha ruler as the new ascendant. Continuing with Saturn's dasha, Saturn is in Taurus so the ascendant ruler becomes Venus, which is in own sign. Saturn now rules the benefic 9th house and the energetic 10th, so it has the potential to be very positive, and in this case it certainly came through for me.

During Saturn-Sun, Saturn-Moon and Saturn-Mars I had several problems, though; in fact, neither of the three planets is a friend of Saturn. On the plus side, I completed my PhD in Cambridge and, most importantly, I started practising yoga and meditation – which changed my life.

In Saturn-Rahu, again with the help of Rahu, I went abroad, circling the globe. I spent a few months in Asia and finally landed in USA. In Saturn-Rahu-Jupiter the expansive energy of Jupiter, this time positive thanks to my meditation practice, brought me some material prosperity, and also a visit to several holy places, first in India and then in Los Angeles at Yogananda's shrines. My meditation practice had improved my response to Saturn. Saturn rules my 7th house, which is occupied by Mars, the 9th ruler, so the 7th house was also active: I met my wife and I made very good spiritual friends in Los Angeles.

In Saturn-Rahu-Saturn I think the contractive energy of Saturn became excessive again, so I had difficulties at work (Saturn is in the 10th house).

Saturn's dasha, like anything related to Saturn, can feel heavy, an almost constant struggle. But it can also be profound, if we are spiritual, and bring inner peace. I've come to appreciate Saturn, but I still blame him, mostly joking, for any difficulty that comes along. I have spent many years under its influence in Saturn's dasha, and I have about three years left before the change to Mercury's dasha – to which I sometimes look forward. The attitude of Mars and Aries is to push through, as I once proved to Drupada, not too seriously, when he asked me about Saturn: "Another three years and he's out of my life!" But as he remarked in response, I might then be relaxing having tea with Mercury, and Saturn would show up as Mercury's friend and guest. There's no escaping Saturn except through spiritual freedom, then there's no reason to avoid him anymore as he becomes a friend.

Sri Yukteswar said that when a devotee is in perfect attunement to God, his actions will naturally be timed according to astrological law, adding: "After deep prayer and meditation he is in touch with his divine consciousness; there is no greater power than that inward protection." Masters are perfectly free and not bound by any star, but sometimes we are able to clearly see that even their actions are in tune with astrological timings. Yogananda was born in Ketu dasha; he starts his autobiography narrating how, when he was still a child, he remembered past lifetimes as a meditating monk.

Ketu is the planet that holds a record of our past, that is why he represents an area in our chart where our habits are especially strong and familiar, and why Rahu, in the opposite and complementary sign, is the direction of new energy and growth.

The next dasha for Yogananda was Venus, which is in his 4th house in Scorpio. The 4th house is the search for inner happiness, a theme central to Yogananda. He came already liberated, but he was setting an example for us, on how to search for our true happiness. By extension, the 4th house represents inner development and general education, like that of childhood. In his autobiography he recounts his profound desire, even as a child, for spiritual happiness. Venus is in Scorpio, a mystical sign which likes to research hidden areas of knowledge. Venus rules the 3rd house of motivated energy and writing, as well as the 10th of public life and work. All these meanings combine to indicate how he was always interested (Venus as the 3rd house ruler) in meeting new saints (Scorpio) and later wrote many stories (3rd house) about those experiences.

In Venus dasha he also began teaching in an official manner by establishing a yoga school for children in India, creating a spiritual home for their inner development – Venus, the teacher planet, in Scorpio in the 4th house.

I think it was during the Venus-Mercury period that Yogananda talked to a Maharaja about the material resources necessary for that yoga school. Mercury is in the 5th house of teaching; it rules the 11th of community as well as the 2nd, a supporting artha house for material resources. The 11th is also the house of gains, and although he didn't personally gain from it, he did secure financial backing.

The school actually began during Venus-Ketu, with only seven kids in a beautiful, remote location. Ketu is in the dynamic 3rd house, which becomes activated in Ketu's sub-period. Ketu likes solitude.

Not long after, Yogananda entered his Sun dasha: the school moved to a new, larger location and attracted hundreds of enrollment requests – the Sun visibly shining. In his chart, the Sun rules the ascendant and is in the 5th house of teaching, in both natal and navamsha charts. In natal chart it is in Sagittarius, in navamsha in Scorpio – inspiring magnetism.

Yogananda moved to USA in Sun-Rahu. Rahu is in the 9th house in Aries, the sign of beginnings; its ruler is Mars, which is in the 8th house in Pisces, a friendly strong sign occupied by Jupiter.

In astrology Sun and Moon are considered enemies of Rahu

Chapter Twenty Five

and Ketu, and indeed when together there can be difficulties. However, when interpreting the meaning of dashas and planets, we need to be or become aware, to some extent, of the level of spiritual attunement of that person. With that awareness we can better understand the degree of harmony between planets.

The Sun, in its highest expression, is the light of pure knowledge, and sharing of that knowledge: Leo is the 5th sign of the natural zodiac, related to the 5th house of dharmic knowledge and teaching. The Moon's highest expression is divine bliss and joy: watery Cancer is the 4th sign of the natural zodiac, interested in inner happiness.

Rahu and Ketu also have spiritual expressions but they are more difficult to manifest, so they can be challenging planets. Because Sun and Moon are, after the ascendant, the most important points in a chart, they are considered especially troubled by Rahu and Ketu.

And yet, there is a subtle connection that unites Sun and Moon with Rahu and Ketu. To either side of our inner spine there are two astral energy channels, called ida and pingala. I referred to these, earlier, simply as the outer part of the inner spine. Ida is associated with Rahu, inhalation, and the upward flow of energy; pingala with Ketu, exhalation, and the downward flow. The ida channel is also related to the Moon, and pingala to the Sun. Sri Yukteswar said that ida is the door of meditation, bringing cheerfulness; pingala is the door of knowledge: when the mind is still, knowledge is revealed.

The calm interiorization of a positive Ketu brings insight and knowledge, like the Sun: Ketu can be like hidden fire, in fact it is strong in fiery Sagittarius. A positive Rahu is active and engaged, even during meditation; it is an upward flow of life-affirming energy, bringing a happy state of mind like a strong Moon.

In their highest expression, Sun and Moon are in harmony with Rahu and Ketu, but until a yogi reaches the level of a master, the response to their combination can be a mixture of good and bad. An astrologer wants to understand the positive and negative aspects of that response, to become more aware of both.

For Yogananda, Sun-Rahu marked the beginning of his mission to the West, to bring the light of knowledge and wisdom to a

Vimshottari dasha

country as restless as Rahu. Rahu marked his move abroad as well as his selfless work. Sun and Rahu are not friends, so for almost anyone else they would have meant some troubles. Rahu is ambitious so it could make Sun too proud and willful. For a master, though, Sun and Rahu are friends. It is interesting, however, that he did have difficulties during that time, in a way, as he had to work tirelessly to spread his teachings, while living with no possessions. He joked that in India disciples bring money to their master, but in USA he had to provide for his disciples. In any case, he was always unaffected by any outward difficulty. He was always joyful, so Sun-Rahu was not a difficult time for him in the same way as it might be difficult for us, if our current dasha was Sun-Rahu.

That is why we should be careful in reading a chart, much depends on whom the chart is describing. The more astrological rules and techniques we learn, the more we should remember that accurate interpretation is only possible through true intuition, attunement to God, and receptivity.

Chapter Twenty Six

Transits

The planets travel all the time through the constellations in the sky, causing their influence to constantly change. The configuration of the stars when we are born is especially influential, but the actual current configuration, and the way it interacts with our chart, are also important. When a planet, in its continuous motion, is going through a sign, it is said to be transiting that sign. A planetary transit will energize that sign and house in our chart. Another effect is that, if a planet is currently transiting in a strong sign, it will also give additional strength to its natal position, even if it's a different sign.

The planets that spend more time in one sign – Jupiter, Saturn, and the lunar nodes – have the most evident transits. By comparison the other planets move quickly through the zodiac so their influence on any one sign is rather temporary. However, in special circumstances their effect can also be noticeable. For example, in 2009 and 2010 Mars went retrograde in Cancer, and instead of the usual two it remained there for several months. I had a friend with Cancer ascendant, with natal Mars in the 10th house in Aries; the effect of the transit on her ascendant was quite evident. Mars is debilitated in Cancer and it can make our emotions too strong, as well as make us feel frustrated as if our life is not progressing. However, it can also be a positive planet for Cancer ascendant as it rules the benefic 5th house and the dynamic 10th house.

She tried the Hong-Sau meditation technique for the first time and right away saw some colored astral lights – something not very common. She has Jupiter in the 9th house in Pisces so she has receptivity, but Mars in Aries is strong in projecting its will; I think during the transit in Cancer Mars became more receptive, giving her a spiritual experience. I don't know if she continued

Transits

meditating, but even if she didn't, that spiritual seed remains in her mind, ready to sprout in a favorable occasion.

Transits can also be helpful in analyzing dashas: when Kriyananda founded the Ananda community in Gurgaon, during his Jupiter-Venus dasha, Jupiter was exalted in that year until July. For a few days Jupiter was together with Venus in Cancer, then later they were together in Leo. In Kriyananda's chart, Jupiter is in the 9th house and Venus is exalted in the 10th. The two benefic planetary teachers came together during that time, both by dasha and by transit.

The dashas are our own personal astrological weather, while the transits give the same weather for everyone, though we will respond to it differently, depending on our own free will and on the specifics of our charts.

Wherever a planet is, in the sky, it is transiting one of our houses, activating it. As another example, Adelle immigrated to USA in her Saturn-Venus-Rahu period. At that time, Saturn was transiting her 12th house together with Jupiter, while Rahu was in Cancer. The 12th house can signify foreign countries and the dasha ruler was transiting it. Cancer is similar to the 4th house so it can indicate home, and Rahu likes change – a change of home. The energy confluence of Saturn and Rahu, both by transit and by dasha, indicated a change of country, and it was strong enough to manifest on the physical plane.

Apart from transiting our houses, the planets also go through a cycle starting the moment we take our first breath. The most important cycles are, again, those of the slower planets – Jupiter, Saturn and the lunar nodes. These cycles are called returns, as these planets move through the zodiac and after a number of years they will return to their initial position in the chart.

Especially important are Jupiter's returns: Yogananda said that we progress in cycles of 12 years, according to the time it takes for Jupiter to return to its natal position. When it does so, it will carry the energy of a new beginning. We might be able to feel this in the mood it encourages but also in factual happenings.

When Adelle went to Ananda to learn meditation, it was a favorable interaction of the natal position of the planets,

Chapter Twenty Six

the dasha, and the transits:

1. Natal Mercury is in receptive Pisces in the 11th house of community. Venus is in Aquarius, a sign of knowledge. Natal Mercury is also with Rahu, which encourages change, and a strong Jupiter in its own sign.

2. The time period was Mercury-Mercury-Venus. Mercury's energy, still at the beginning phase of its dasha, was new, quick and light. The 3rd level ruler was the benefic teacher Venus, Mercury's planetary friend.

3. Jupiter was transiting Pisces, which was an especially strong and favorable moment because her natal Jupiter is in Pisces – it was her Jupiter return. Venus was transiting Libra, a social sign seeking inner harmony. Saturn, the natal 9th ruler, was in Virgo, the sign of yoga techniques. Rahu was transiting Sagittarius, the natal 8th house of transformation. Mercury was in Leo, her 4th house – learning meditation at Ananda was a search for inner happiness (4th house) as well as strength and confidence of mind (Mercury in Leo).

This planetary confluence by dasha, transit and natal position was certainly life changing.

The other two important returns are those of Saturn, which take about 29 years, and of the lunar nodes, which happen every 18 years and some months. Saturn transits are influential not only at the time of its returns, but especially when it transits either the ascendant or the Moon. In fact, the transit on the Moon is considered in an expanded way: not only on the natal Moon, but also on the sign before and after, for a total of about 7 years. This period is called Sade Sati and it is a time when Saturn is taking a special interest in us. The Moon is our state of mind, so with Saturn our mind can become anything but peaceful, and feel very heavy. However, Sade Sati can also be an intensely spiritual time. As always, with any combination of Saturn and Moon it is better to keep our mind busy with wholesome activities, so that no energy is left for brooding and worrying, the negative effects of Saturn on the Moon.

When Saturn is strong, we can feel responsible for the consequences of every action and thought, but, once we do our best, we should let go of that sense of responsibility and leave everything in the much more capable hands of God – that's karma yoga. If the thought of letting go makes us worry that we haven't really done our best, then it is safe to say that we are worrying too much. Yogananda said to be calmly active and actively calm. Work does not need to equate stress: if we have the right attitude we can be calm at work too.

Saturn is the planet of concentration, so when it transits the ascendant we might find a new focus and direction in life. My Moon is in the 11th house, so I happen to have both of Saturn's main transits consecutively, first Sade Sati and then on the ascendant: I had several years of Saturn focusing on an important point in my chart. Additionally, my recent Saturn transits occurred during Saturn dasha. On top of that, my natal Saturn is strong in the 10th house. It hasn't always been easy, but overall Saturn has brought me many gifts, for which I am grateful. It really changed my life for the better.

Saturn often signifies difficulties so, if we remember that, we can plan accordingly. For example, for 20 years I had excellent health, but during my Saturn-Rahu period Saturn entered Libra, and Mars entered Leo. Saturn and Rahu can be the most difficult planetary combination, and they are together in Virgo in my navamsha, on the ascendant. The ascendant can indicate physical vitality and Virgo is the mutable earth sign, very sensitive to physical environment. Although Mars is a benefic planet in my natal chart, ruling the 9th house, it is in general a planet that can cause problems – though not usually as bad as Saturn. Mars is not a natural benefic like Jupiter and Venus.

Saturn and Mars were transiting the signs on either side of Virgo, a constrictive influence. The dasha and the transits combined to give me a bad case of sinus infection. If I had understood the astrological conditions I could have been more careful, instead I went outside in winter not well covered and got sick. Normally colds don't affect me that much but I had spent the previous months in a stressful situation, so my aura was already weakened. I was feeling quite miserable and I could not even meditate; at one point, though, I was able to be receptive to divine grace and I gradually improved.

Yogananda explained that ultimately all diseases are rooted in our consciousness. They start in the mind as diseased thoughts, and if they gain strength they eventually manifest as physical illnesses. By a strong thought of affirmative health we can immediately, or gradually, get rid of any disease, depending on the strength of our willpower and receptivity to grace.

The lunar nodes returns can be an interesting time of our life, if not always easy. Their natal houses will be especially active. The night my recent nodes return started I had a vivid spiritual dream. My natal nodes are in the 5th and 11th house, and during the year and a half they spent in their natal signs I had many intense experiences. Some experiences were of Rahu nature, some of Ketu, and others a balanced blend of the two; they were especially related to spiritual knowledge (5th house) and community (11th house).

I graduated and left Cambridge. I spent some time at Ananda in Assisi, where San Francis lived and was buried. I lived in South Korea for a winter; hardly anyone spoke english there and I felt rather isolated, so I clung to the thought of God every moment, and had a joyful Christmas in meditation. I visited some Ananda centers and many of Yogananda's shrines, in India and in Los Angeles. I made wonderful spiritual friends and met my wife. I had a few challenging moments, but often I felt very close to Yogananda.

Now my nodes are transiting the 3rd and 9th houses of my navamsha, a good time to write a book on spiritual astrology. My Sun is exalted in the natal 9th house, and in navamsha it is in Scorpio in the 3rd house: Rahu transiting Scorpio is activating Scorpio and the Sun with a specific focus.

Rahu likes change and I certainly experienced a lot of change during its return. On the other hand, Rahu has energy but is not easily stable or consistent. For example, during a Rahu dasha we might feel unsettled. The dasha following Rahu's would be Jupiter's; if Jupiter is strong in the natal chart, Jupiter's dasha would give a sense of increased inner stability, compared to the preceding dasha. Similarly, if Rahu is transiting an important point in our chart, like the Moon, it might make us restless. But if we are aware of that, we can channel its active energy into some creative project rather than let it affect us in a negative way.

As another example of house activation, when Rahu transited my natal 9th house of higher education I went abroad to continue my university studies. Then it went into the 8th house of transformation, during Saturn's transit on the Moon, and I certainly felt as if my life had started anew.

Interpreting dashas and transits is an advanced technique, as we need first a solid understanding of the influence of those planets in their original positions in the natal and navamsha charts. Dashas and transits can be used to make predictions by a good astrologer, but Sri Yukteswar said that the stars only show the probable future, which our free will can change. Yogananda said: "Seeds of past karma cannot germinate if they are roasted in the divine fires of wisdom."

In India you can get a predictive reading made for you a long time ago, before any of us were born. The authentic ones are said to have been made by a sage like Agasthya or Brighu; to preserve them they are rewritten on new leaves every few hundred years. Kriyananda had a few such readings and they were uncanningly exact in several things. I had an Agasthya reading in the same center and it foretold I would be married in about a year, which I did not believe at the time, but it came true. Other predictions of my reading are more ambiguous and I don't think they have or will materialize. I believe there's a difference between things we want (like getting married) and things we don't want; provided our choice is done with discrimination, our efforts and divine grace will help us realize one and not the other.

Chapter Twenty Six

In any case, Kriyananda's reading says he will leave his body at the age of 91, or it could be 90 as India's calendar is a little different – that's around the time Saturn will transit its natal position, which happens every 29 years. I wouldn't be surprised if Kriyananda left at that time, as Yogananda did the same. As Drupada observed, Yogananda left his body at the exact moment of both Jupiter and Saturn returns, which happened on the 7th of March 1952. Kriyananda's exact Saturn return will happen in 2014 at the beginning of Scorpio. Saturn will remain in Scorpio until 2017, when he will be 91. It will then move into Sagittarius and return briefly in Scorpio still in 2017. Kriyananda has dedicated his whole life to continuing the work started by his guru, and maybe he will leave in a similar manner to rejoin him in Infinite Bliss.

Chapter Twenty Seven

Positional strength

Planets are stronger in the four angular houses, but they also have a preferred house along the two main axis formed by the 1st and 7th houses, and the 4th and 10th.

Sun and Mars are fiery and self-confident: they are stronger in the 10th, a house of strength and visibility. The 10th is also said to be the south direction, where Sun is generally warmer and brighter. Now, east and west have the same symbolism everywhere on Earth, as the rising and setting direction of the Sun. However, to identify the 10th as south and the 4th as north is correct only in the northern hemisphere, where the constellations of the zodiac are visible in the south direction.

The zodiac is a ring around the Earth, and only part of it is visible in the sky at any one time. The sign that is highest in the visible sky is in the south direction in the northern hemisphere and in the north direction in the southern hemisphere.

The 10th house is a house of visibility, so we can identify the visible part of the zodiac as the 10th house, while the hidden side is the 4th. In the northern hemisphere the 10th house is then identified with the south, while in the southern hemisphere with the north.

Astrology tradition comes from India, in the northern hemisphere, however it makes sense for me as I was born in Europe. For me, south is the direction of summer, an outgoing season when nature is in full expression, while north is the direction of winter, a time for introspection. To be more precise, we can simply consider the 10th as the direction towards the warmer climates of the equator, where the Sun becomes stronger, and the 4th as towards the cold weather of the frozen poles, preserving the symbolism in both hemispheres.

Chapter Twenty Seven

Moon and Venus are stronger in the 4th, the house of inner reality and happiness: both are sensitive, receptive planets. The 4th is the direction away from the equator where the light is generally cooler, more soothing and less scorching, and neither Moon nor Venus are fiery.

Saturn is stronger in the 7th, the house furthest away from us: it is the planet of the earth chakra representing the point furthest away from Spirit. The 7th is west, opposite the most spiritual cardinal point: the east. East is the 1st house, symbolizing the rising light, while the west is the descending light, heralding the darkness of the material world. West is the direction of autumn, when the light of the Sun is declining towards winter, a more sober and serious mood than summer or spring. In many climates, flowers are nearly absent in autumn and leaves are falling.

Mercury and Jupiter are stronger in the 1st house. Jupiter represents guru and is the most benefic planet; it is happy in the most benefic cardinal point. Mercury is the son of Jupiter and the planet of the ether chakra, it likes to be further away from the physical materiality of the west. Mercury can be involved with the material world but it is etheric, never as materially heavy as Saturn. East is the direction of spring, when things are light, quick and young, just like Mercury.

Positional strength, or digbala in sanskrit, doesn't overrule the more important concepts of angular houses and sign rulership. A planet in an angular house, in own sign, or exalted is always energetic regardless of digbala.

Digbala houses are all angular. The strongest angular house is the 10th, followed in order by the 7th, 4th and 1st. Each planet will be slightly stronger than normal in its favorite angular house, but the 10th remains always the most energetic. Positional strength is a subtle refinement in understanding how comfortable a planet is in a house, not crucial, but possibly helpful.

Chapter Twenty Eight

Planetary yogas

Yogas are specific placements of planets with a codified interpretation which describes their likely effects. The same meanings of virtually every yoga can be derived directly just by interpreting the chart, without using these codified rules, however it is useful to understand the underlying principle of a yoga formulation. There are hundreds of yogas and some are elaborate and esoteric, taking into account several planets, their position by sign and by house, and the position of the planet which rules the sign they occupy. The planet which rules the sign that another planet occupies is called its dispositor. For example, if the Sun is in Aries its dispositor is Mars. The strength of Mars influences that of its sign Aries, so indirectly also the strength of the Sun.

A rather involved yoga example is Kalpadruma yoga, which considers four planets: 1. the ascendant ruler; 2. its dispositor; 3. the dispositor of planet 2; 4. the navamsha dispositor of planet 3. For this yoga to occur, all these planets must be in an angular or trine house, or be exalted. For example, take my chart: 1. Sun is exalted; 2. Mars is in 7th house; 3. Saturn is in 10th house; 4. Mercury is in 9th house, so I have Kalpadruma yoga. Kalpadruma means wish-fulfilling tree and is supposed to be an auspicious yoga, which is nice to know. However, its description doesn't give any additional information on how the planets interact, or what we can do to improve it. In my life I had much difficult karma and many blessings, and we've already analyzed some of the positive and challenging interactions of those four planets in my chart. Kalpadruma yoga seems to indicate they will eventually come together in a positive way, but all planets gradually do for a yogi. This is why I consider the system of planetary yogas as one of the many possible alternative methods for chart interpretation, and

Chapter Twenty Eight

not an essential tool. It is probably more important in predictive astrology, as combining yogas and dashas can help in timing specific results with more accuracy.

It is evident that an underlying principle of Kalpadruma yoga is that the strength of a dispositor affects the strength of a planet, and we can continue in that direction by looking at the dispositor of the dispositor, and even consider the potential to improve by looking at the navamsha.

Other yogas are based on how positive or negative planets, placed on either side of a sign, can improve on, or detract from, the strength of the sign in the middle. Many yogas look at the house placement relative to the ascendant or Moon. For example, Gaja Kesari yoga is formed when Jupiter is in an angular house from the Moon or the ascendant, if supported by benefic planets, and not weakened by being combust, debilitated or in the sign of an enemy. The underlying principle of Gaja Kesari yoga is that Jupiter is a generally benefic planet, and if it is in a strong house from the Moon it indicates positive energy in the chart. Gaja Kesari yoga shows material and mental prosperity.

By using the same principle of this yoga, we can also check if Jupiter is in an angular house from the ascendant, or the Sun. If Gaja Kesari, or any other yoga, recurs from all ascendants, it will be stronger.

To evaluate the strength of a yoga we need to see if the planets that form it are supported or afflicted by the rest of the chart. We can also check if any of the yoga planets are ruling a dasha or making an important transit – that's when the yoga could manifest its effects. Probably my Kalpadruma yoga will not materialize in an evident manner until Mercury's dasha. This is because Saturn brings delays, and it is rather strong in the 10th house in rashi chart; it is also on the navamsha ascendant. Saturn improves with time as we learn to respond to it in a better way. It is the planet that especially shows attachments and worries. Attachment is the fear of losing something, while a worry is the fear that something might or might not happen. A yogi gradually learns to let go of fear, and surrenders to divine grace – then Saturn becomes the planet of loyalty, steadfastness and peace.

The most simple yogas are rather straightforward to understand: they are formed when either Mercury, Venus, Mars, Jupiter or Saturn is in own sign or in exaltation, and either in an angular or trine house. Such planet will be strong by sign, and either energetic (in an angular) or benefic (in a trine) by house. However, we still need to interpret each yoga in a specific chart. For example, my Venus is in Taurus in the 10th house, so it forms a Venus yoga, but Saturn casts a strong shadow on it. If my Venus yoga were without any kind of negative affliction it would be much stronger.

If we are able to understand and interpret the position and interactions of the planets in a chart, then yogas aren't really necessary, however there is a special class which is based on a rather important principle: the Raja yogas. These are formed when there is a combination of angular and trine houses, energy and grace; angular houses have energy and trine houses direct it in a benefic way. Raja yogas form with several such combinations, for example if a ruler of an angular house and the ruler of a trine house are together, either in a trine or in an angular house. Another possible combination is if an angular ruler and a trine ruler are each in the sign ruled by the other, while still in a trine or angular house. This is called a sign exchange or mutual reception. A sign exchange, or Parivartana yoga, always shows a strengthening and coming together of two planets, even when it doesn't involve angular or trine houses, so this kind of Raja yoga is a special case of Parivartana.

The stronger Raja yogas are formed when the 9th and 10th houses are involved, but all of them are auspicious.

A special case of Raja yoga is formed when a planet rules both a trine and an angular house, in which case it assumes an especially benefic role, and it is called Raja yoga karaka (karaka means significator). Only half of the ascendants have a Raja yoga karaka: for Leo and Cancer it is Mars; for Taurus and Libra it is Saturn; for Capricorn and Aquarius it is Venus.

For example, Mars is in my 7th house, forming a Raja yoga by

Chapter Twenty Eight

itself, because it rules the 4th and 9th houses for Leo ascendants. The interpretation of Mars in my chart is not really changed by this fact, but now we know that Mars has an extra bit of strength and positive energy.

I mentioned before how I moved to Cambridge in Saturn-Venus-Saturn, and we briefly analyzed that part of Saturn's dasha by using the technique of making the dasha ruler as a new ascendant. For that dasha, Taurus becomes the ascendant. Saturn is Raja yoga karaka for Taurus, and in the 1st house it forms a strong Raja yoga, making Saturn-Venus-Saturn a favorable period, thanks to the softening influence of Venus.

Yogas seen from the ascendant show factual events, while looking at them from the Moon focuses on how we feel about what is happening. However, the mind is also important in influencing material reality, so if strong yogas happen both from the ascendant and from the Moon we can take it as a confirmation of their importance. If the same yoga exists from the ascendant, the Moon, and the Sun, it will be very strong.

When I attended an astrology class by Drupada, the chart for that day had some strong Raja yogas favorable for studying astrology. The ascendant was Leo and was occupied by Mars and Venus. Mars is the Raja yoga karaka and Venus the ruler of the 10th house. Mars alone forms a Raja yoga. Mars with Venus also forms a Raja yoga, of the strongest kind as it involves the 9th and 10th rulers.

Additionally, Moon and Jupiter were in Pisces, forming a Raja yoga from the Moon: taking Pisces as ascendant, the Moon rules the 5th house, while Jupiter rules the 1st and 10th. This yoga from the Moon was in the 8th house from the Leo ascendant, a good house for astrology and for studying spiritual subjects.

As an example of how to time the fruition of yogas with the dashas, lets consider again my Kalpadruma yoga, formed by Sun, Mars, Saturn and Mercury.

So far I have been through Rahu's dasha, then Jupiter's, and now

Planetary yogas

I'm near the end of Saturn's. In Rahu's dasha I was just a child, and we expect delays from Saturn in my Kalpadruma yoga, so it's unlikely it'd manifest during childhood. Considering Jupiter's dasha, Jupiter is debilitated and in any case does not participate in this yoga, making it unlikely as well. Saturn's dasha is probably also not a good time: Saturn is delaying the yoga and is not a natural friend of the ascendant. That makes Mercury's dasha the earliest candidate. We would then look at a sub-period in this dasha, either ruled by Sun, which is exalted in the 9th house, or by Mars, which is also forming a Raja yoga. For instance, Mercury-Sun-Mars or Mercury-Mars-Sun. Probably Saturn would have to be in there as well, by transit or sub-period, and I'll get a cookie, or something.

Chapter Twenty Nine

Gems and mantras

A primary purpose of astrology is to understand our energetic habits, in order to improve our strengths and change any bad habit that affects our happiness. In addition to meditation and other yoga techniques, there are two methods that are quite effective in strengthening our aura: gems and mantras. Mantras are combinations of sanskrit words which are specific to a certain type of consciousness we want to attune with. The most straightforward mantras are those dedicated to the nine planets. For example, my Jupiter is debilitated so I chant a mantra for Jupiter every day. Normally mantras are chanted for 108 times (or more, if you like), a number which has special significance in astrology: 12 signs times 9 planets equals 108. I started doing the mantra only on Thursdays, the day of Jupiter, but eventually I increased the frequency.

Other mantras are dedicated to deities. For example, a mantra for Ganesha is good to find wisdom and remove obstacles. Mantras should be intoned correctly, so you have to hear them; it is not too helpful to read them unless you know a little about sanskrit pronunciation. I guess the International Phonetic Alphabet could work to write them down, but it's not an alphabet which is widely known. Also, to choose the correct mantra one has to be able to reliably interpret a chart. Normally the mantras most indicated are those for the three rulers of the benefic trine houses, however it also depends on the natural character of that planet. For instance, my ascendant ruler is the Sun, which is exalted, so I don't do any mantra for the Sun – it could increase its fire excessively. If my ascendant ruler was exalted Jupiter I might still do a mantra to increase its energy, because Jupiter is benefic. If Saturn rules one of the trines we must exercise caution with its mantra, but with

Gems and mantras

the right spirit it could be good for concentration and self-control.

Another way to strengthen the planets is to wear gems. Similarly to the mantras, gems are usually indicated only for the rulers of the trine houses. Since those three houses have the same element, one normally wears gems that belong to either one of the two elemental families: fire and water (Sun, Moon, Mars and Jupiter), or air and earth (Saturn, Venus and Mercury). The specific chart might warrant some exceptions, allowing some mixing between the two groups. For example, if the Moon is in a difficult placement, it might be a good idea to wear a pearl, even if your ascendant is in an air or earth sign.

Astrological gems must be of the highest quality and of certain weight. I would not advice anyone to buy them in a normal jewelry shop as gems will be grossly overpriced, and their color enhanced by irradiation or chemical treatment. It is best to buy them from a trustworthy astrological dealer. Special care is needed also when setting them into a jewel.

Each planet has a primary gem, and several secondary gems which are usually cheaper but less powerful. The primary gem for Jupiter is yellow sapphire; the secondary gems are other yellow crystals, the cheapest of which is citrine quartz. I had a 12 carat citrine in a bangle until I was able to afford a sapphire. Jupiter rules my 5th house so it is positive for me. I also used to wear a red coral, the gem for Mars. Mars rules my 9th house so it is a benefic trine ruler, but it is also fiery, so if I wore a big coral it might make me too temperamental. My wife has strong fire planets, so at times I wouldn't even wear a coral at all, as I had plenty of fiery energy mixing into my aura because of her company, in addition to my exalted Sun. Also, when Mars was strong by transit, maybe spending time in Aries or Leo, then its energy would be higher and I felt I didn't need to strengthen it further. Eventually I stopped wearing coral altogether.

For a short while I also had a Rahu gem, because my Moon is with Ketu, making Ketu quite influential; the Rahu gem was helping with balancing the lunar nodes. Wearing the gems for the nodes should be done with caution.

The reason I used to wear a coral is that my Mars is aspected

175

Chapter Twenty Nine

by Saturn, through its special aspect: Mars is in the 10th house from Saturn. To not increase its fire too much, I set it in silver, which cools the coral and makes it more mellow. My sapphire, instead, is set in gold to enhance its energy. The gold amount in the alloy also matters. I have it in 18 kt gold, while Adelle has set her emerald in 14 kt gold. Jupiter rules a fire sign and is a friend of Mars and Sun so it likes fire, but it is better to not make Mercury too fiery.

It is also possible to wear a gem for each of the nine planets, in a bangle called navaratna. However, the relative strength of the gems in a navaratna still needs to be tailored to each person.

The primary gems for the other seven planets are: diamond for Venus; blue sapphire for Saturn; ruby for Sun; pearl for Moon; emerald for Mercury; chrysoberyl for Ketu; hessonite for Rahu. The secondary gems are simply other crystals of the same color, for example white sapphire for Venus and green tourmaline for Mercury.

Gems should be worn touching the skin, and in my experience the strongest way would be as a ring, but each gem must go on a specific finger. Jupiter and Sun should be worn on the index finger; Venus and Saturn on the middle finger; Mars on the ring finger; Mercury on the middle or little finger. Normally rings are worn on the right hand, which projects energy into action, but can be worn on the left, which is more receptive.

Sometimes a gem of a planet which does not rule a trine can be indicated: Swami Kriyananda wears a Jupiter ring to strengthen his 10th house because he needs a lot of energy for his public work; this was also suggested in his Agasthya reading. In my Agasthya reading it says I should wear an emerald, which rules the 11th and 2nd houses, so it is not a gem we would prescribe by the normal rules of astrology. Probably it is a suggestion to strengthen my Moon as it is in a difficult position with Ketu. In fact I have tried briefly wearing an emerald and I felt some extra clarity of mind. On the other hand, Mercury rules a house of kama, the 11th; kama signifies desires so increasing its energy can increase our desires.

As another chart example we can take Kate's (on page 116): it

Gems and mantras

is good for her to wear a gem for Mercury, the ruler of the 9th house, and for Venus, the ascendant ruler. Saturn rules her 4th and 5th and it is a trine ruler as well as Raja yoga karaka, so wearing a Saturn gem could be good, but only when she is ready to handle its energy, otherwise it could decrease her vitality. Saturn is with Sun in Leo and the Sun indicates vitality. Although the Sun is strong in her chart, if we increase Saturn's energy, and we are not responding to it in a good way, it would constrict the light of the Sun. The ascendant also indicates vitality and its ruler Venus is debilitated, so we must be careful.

Drupada suggested for her to chant a mantra for Durga, the warrior aspect of Divine Mother. Durga will give her protection and empowerment. Kate has a prominent 12th house, where the ascendant ruler is debilitated. With that combination we can be compassionate and sensitive, like the 12th sign of the natural zodiac, Pisces. In the 12th house we learn to be channels of God to share His energy. If we act as a channel we will be energized, but if instead of channeling we give our energy away, we will feel depleted.

Kriyananda once was told by Yogananda to greet comers to their Sunday service by shaking hands. Afterwards, Kriyananda had felt tired, so Yogananda explained he should not give of his own energy, but rather be a channel of divine energy. Kate can chant Durga's mantra to protect her aura so that she is not weakened while teaching her numerous classes.

For a similar reason, Durga's mantra is very appropriate for Adelle because she has Rahu, Jupiter and debilitated Mercury in Pisces. Another good mantra for her is that for the Moon, though it is not a trine ruler. Adelle's Moon is debilitated in Scorpio and Mars aspects it from Taurus opposite. Taurus is a rather patient sign, but Scorpio and Mars are not, so their projection of energy on the Moon, which represents our state of mind, can make us impatient and a bit fiery. Soma is the gentle deity of the Moon and a mantra dedicated to Soma can calm her feelings and reinforce her patience.

As a corollary to wearing gems, the color of our clothing and the predominant colors in our home can also be influential. For

Chapter Twenty Nine

example, Saturn is too strong in my chart. Its gem is blue sapphire, so I should never wear it (other than in a navaratna), and I should also not wear blue or black, unless very occasionally. If I became a Nayaswami, wearing royal blue would be fine, because it would have a special spiritual significance.

Jupiter's colors are yellow and orange, which are warm and kind. Venus likes white and pastel colors. Moon prefers white, while Sun and Mars obviously go for red. Mercury's color is green. Wearing colors is not nearly as strong as wearing gems, so it is fine to wear colors of any planet, generally speaking, maybe with the exception of Saturn which is the most problematic planet, and perhaps red if your chart is too fiery.

For some strange reason we are often attracted to those very colors and gems which are not good for us: before I got an astrological reading I used to wear only blue and black almost every day.

Yogananda also suggested wearing an astrological bangle made of three intertwined strands of copper, silver and gold. Copper should stand for the physical body, or the ascendant; silver for the mind, or Moon; and gold for the soul, or Sun. These bangles are prepared following a specific formula and are very effective at energizing our aura.

If you meditate, practice yoga at all times, wear gems and chant mantras, and you still feel overwhelmed by difficulties, do not give up! Listen to Yogananda:

"If failures invade you repeatedly, don't get discouraged. They should act as stimulants and not poisons to your material or spiritual growth. The period of failure is the best season for sowing the seeds of success. Weed out the causes of failure and launch with double vigor what you want to accomplish. The bludgeon of circumstances may bleed you but keep your head unbowed. Death in the attempt to succeed is success; refuse to harbor the consciousness of defeat. Try always once more, no matter how many times you have failed. Persevere one minute more in the race for success when you and all have done their best and can do no more. Fight when you think you can fight no more or when you think that you have fought to your best. Every new effort after a failure must be well planned and charged

Gems and mantras

with increasing intensity of attention. Begin from today to try to do one at a time the things you thought impossible for you to do. Malignant seeds of past Karma (action) can be roasted only by the fire of persistent effort until they are destroyed. Most people give up hope just when the balance of good Karma slowly stoops toward them to give fruit, and thus miss their reward."

Chapter Thirty

Nakshatras

The nakshatras are also called lunar signs because they have a special importance for the Moon, while the twelve signs are called solar. The lunar signs are simply a division into smaller groups of the same circle of stars that forms the twelve solar signs.

The Sun takes one year to make one full lap around the stars, and normally during this time the Moon has twelve phase cycles, giving origin to the division of the circle of stars into twelve signs. Conversely, the Moon takes about 27 days to make one full lap around the stars. Each of these 27 days is like a phase cycle for the Sun, from dawn through sunset to dawn. Thus, an alternative division of the same circle of stars, through which the Moon and Sun travel, is into 27 groups instead of 12.

In both cases, to determine the number of solar or lunar signs we count the number of cycles one planet goes through, during the time necessary for the other planet to go one full circle around the stars. The Moon goes through 12 Moon-cycles (twelve months) during the time it takes the Sun to make one lap around the stars, so there are twelve solar signs. Conversely, the Sun goes through 27 Sun-cycles (27 days) during the time it takes the Moon to make one lap around the stars, so there are 27 lunar signs, or nakshatras.

The 360 degrees of the full circle of stars, divided into 12 give the solar signs of 30 degrees each, while divided into 27 give the smaller lunar signs of 13 degrees and 20 minutes each.

The Moon goes through all the nakshatras in 27 days and a fraction, spending about a day in each nakshatra. If we listen carefully, each day we might feel some hint of the nakshatra the Moon is transiting, as a subtle influence on our mental outlook. In theory, we can look at the nakshatra position of each planet in a chart, but unless we are doing an extensive and detailed reading it is perfectly fine to just look at the nakshatra of the Moon.

Nakshatras have their own traits and characteristics just like the twelve bigger signs. They are smaller groupings of the same stars that make up the solar signs, so it follows that some qualities of each nakshatra will be present in the solar sign which shares those same stars.

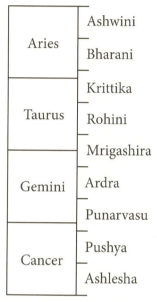

First group of nakshatras. The first nine nakshatras correspond exactly to the first four solar signs.

The beginning of the first nakshatra, Ashwini, coincides with the beginning of Aries, but due to the different length of the solar and lunar signs, some nakshatras are contained fully in a solar sign while others overlap between two. For example, Krittika nakshatra is partly in Aries and partly in Taurus.

Nine nakshatras span exactly the same distance of four signs, so the 27 lunar signs are divided into three groups of nine each. The first group begins with Aries, the second with Leo and the third with Sagittarius.

Each nakshatra is ruled by a planet, starting with Ashwini which is ruled by Ketu. The planetary rulers of the nakshatras follow the same order, repeated three times in total, once for each

Chapter Thirty

group of nine nakshatras. It is the same order we used previously for the vimshottari dasha system: Ketu, Venus, Sun, Moon, Mars, Rahu, Jupiter, Saturn, and Mercury. The reason is that the ruler of the first dasha is the ruler of the nakshatra of our natal Moon. For example, if at our birth the Moon is in Aries, at 3 degrees 20 minutes, it will be in Ashwini (which goes from 0 degrees to 13 degrees 20 minutes). The fraction of the Moon's nakshatra which still remains for the Moon to transit is the fraction of the dasha that still has to unfold. Continuing with our example, 3 degrees 20 minutes are exactly 1/4 of Ashwini. Ashwini is ruled by Ketu, which has a full dasha of 7 years. Since the Moon is at 1/4 of Ashwini, we start the dasha at 1/4 of 7 years, or 1 year and 9 months. At our birth, then, the Moon still has 3/4 to travel in Ashwini, so our Ketu dasha will last 3/4 of its full 7 years. In other words, our Ketu dasha will last until we are 5 years and 3 months old, instead of 7 years old. All the following dashas last for their complete duration, because the Moon has to travel through the complete length of the following nakshatras.

Apart its planetary ruler, each nakshatra has several other attributes, the most notable being a specific deity.

The first nakshatra is *Ashwini* and its deities are the Ashwini twins, sons of the Sun when he was in the form of a stallion. This is the part of Aries that is quick, agile, youthful, ever new. Like an ideal horse it is strong, healthy and energetic. This nakshatra is especially associated with healing, as overcoming an illness feels like a new beginning. The Ashwini twins are considered the healers of the gods with the power to give new life to anyone, but they must exercise wisdom in doing so, to avoid unwise consequences. Yogananda said they are the gods of twilight, heralding dawn, representing light and darkness, the duality of creation.

Ashwini is ruled by Ketu, the planet of non-intellectual insight. Ketu, like Mars, is not a thinking planet, and it represents energy descending from a higher plane. In this sense it symbolizes the beginning of creation and of the zodiac, as light descending to the material plane to create the universe.

Ketu can have a separating influence, and Mars is not known for its innate sensitivity, so their combination can make us insensitive. However, if we are compassionate they can give us some detachment and self-control, needed for a healer to not be overwhelmed by other people's suffering, in order to be able to help them. Sun is exalted in Aries, but its exaltation is stronger in Ashwini than in the rest of the sign – the deities of this nakshatra are the Sun's family. Adelle has Sun in Ashwini and she wants to be a physician, a healer.

The next nakshatra is *Bharani*, ruled by Venus, the planet which shows the things we love. Venus likes creativity and it can be a nurturing planet, as it is softer than Mars. This is the part of Aries which loves to be active, creative and passionately engaged. The deity is Yama, god of Dharma: Bharani shows the dedication needed to stand for dharma against any contrary influence. Yama means control, and Venus is the planet of pranayama: both indicate the need to control our energy and channel it in a constructive way, otherwise our life will be wasted following our desires – then Yama takes on his other meaning as the god of death. On the other hand, death for a yogi is but a new beginning.

Krittika nakshatra is 1/4 in Aries and 3/4 in Taurus, bridging the two signs. Each quarter of a nakshatra is called a pada. Krittika is ruled by Sun and its deity is Agni, god of fire. Its stars are the Pleiades cluster, of which seven are the brightest; in the myth they are sisters who take care of Mars as a child, but his childhood is short, as the little warrior kills a powerful demon when he's just a few days old. This fiery nakshatra shows independence and determination, traits present in both Aries and Taurus, signs which can be very stubborn. Agni as the god of fire is associated with the fire ceremony, where we are purified by the fire of wisdom. Sri Yukteswar, a master renown for his wisdom, had Sun exalted in Krittika.

In the Bhagavad Gita it is said that yoga meditation, like Kriya yoga taught by Yogananda, is a metaphysical fire ceremony, but it is also a pranayama technique. It is not so surprising, then, to find Agni partly in a fire sign and partly in earthy Taurus, a sign which is in the chakra of pranayama. However, the fiery energy and drive of Krittika is expressed in different ways in Aries and Taurus, because each solar sign has a different element, and is

Chapter Thirty

also a mixture of three different nakshatras. In Aries, a fire sign, Krittika's fire is enhanced by Ashwini, a dynamic nakshatra. In Taurus, instead, Krittika is mixed with Rohini, a soft and nurturing nakshatra which calms its fire, giving an overall feel for Taurus which is not fiery but down to earth.

If I had had to pick a Taurus nakshatra as the strongest for the Moon's exaltation, I would have chosen Rohini, but it is actually Krittika. I think one reason is that being a mother, one of the Moon's symbols, is not just about being loving and nurturing, but also fiercely protective. Mothers also need fiery energy to keep up with their kids! The seven sisters, stars of Krittika, were able to take care of Mars, of all kids. I think the Moon is strengthened by the inner stability of mind and will needed for that accomplishment. When a planet is exalted it receives some extra strength that integrates with its normal qualities, making it special. In Krittika, the Moon gains special stability and power.

Rohini is fully in Taurus; it is ruled by gentle Moon and its deity is Prajapati, creator and protector of life, and son of Brahma. This nakshatra is cheerful and relaxed and represents beauty in form, whether pure or sensual. For example, some time ago the Moon was in Rohini; the feel for that day was very nice and we were eating ice-cream under a beautiful blue sky with wandering white clouds.

Rohini is attractive and magnetic: Krishna's Moon and ascendant are in this nakshatra. Adelle has Rohini ascendant and she's beautiful and charming. Rohini is that part of Taurus which is nourishing and beautiful.

The last nakshatra of Taurus is *Mrigashira*, which is also half in Gemini. The primary drive of this nakshatra is searching, a trait shared by Taurus and Gemini in their own way. Taurus looks for stability and Gemini has an enquiring and curious mind.

The Moon spends about a day in each nakshatra. In the evening of the same day I just mentioned about Rohini, Moon changed to Mrigashira and I talked to a friend who was interested in yoga – searching for knowledge.

Mrigashira is ruled by Mars, which gives it energy and drive, and its deity is Soma, sensitivity of perception. Soma also represents bliss, the common denominator of all searches. Kriyananda often repeats that the underlying, sometimes subconscious, motivation of every action is always the search for soul happiness. Unfortunately, this search is all too often directed towards temporary and even deleterious sense happiness, that is why Mrigashira can leave us dissatisfied if we don't have the wisdom to direct our search towards God.

Mrigashira is often translated as head of the deer, from mriga, deer, and shira, head. It is a reference to hunting (searching), and the fact that deer activities are tied to the Moon phases, part of a hunter's knowledge. The month Margashirsha (an auspiciously cool month in India's winter) is said to derive its name from the nakshatra, though some consider it a different spelling (or transliteration) of the same sanskrit word. In the Bhagavad Gita, Krishna says that of all the months he is the most auspicious, Margashirsha, and Yogananda translates it as marga, the divine path to, shirsha, head – in other words, the path to supreme consciousness.

Ardra is fully contained in Gemini and is ruled by Rahu; its deity is Rudra, a form of Shiva and god of storms. Both planet and deity give Ardra intense energy. This nakshatra is inclined to create a storm and can be a little destructive, but its purpose is ambitious: to find true knowledge. In this it is similar to Mrigashira, but Rahu is airy, unlike Mars, and Rudra is very different from Soma. Ardra defines that intense curiosity of Gemini which can become too restless and nerve-wrecking. A symbol for this nakshatra is the diamond, which is born from carbon under intense pressure. Rudra can create a storm in our consciousness with the intention of purifying it, but it does not encourage calmness. Whether positively or negatively directed, the efforts of Ardra need to be balanced with relaxation and inner peace to achieve lightness of mind. Kriyananda's ascendant is in Ardra, like my Ketu and Moon.

The next nakshatra, *Punarvasu*, completes Gemini and has one pada in Cancer; its name means return of the light. It is ruled by Jupiter and its deity is Aditi, the Cosmic Mother of the gods. Jupiter and Aditi are benefic and indicate expansive creativity: Punarvasu can give prosperity, lightness of feeling, and a sense

Chapter Thirty

of natural kinship with others and the universe. Being creative and sociable are common traits of Gemini and Cancer.

Ramana Maharshi had Ketu with Moon in Gemini, but in Punarvasu rather than in Ardra like in my chart. Ketu with Moon in Gemini is questioning and spiritual but also destabilizing. It is certainly easier to deal with in benefic Punarvasu, rather than in the storm created by Ardra. Of course there are other factors to account for the difference. Gemini is his 9th house, while for me it is the 11th house. He was also a very advanced yogi, as it is said he attained liberation at the age of 16.

Pushya is fully in Cancer; it is ruled by Saturn and its deity is Brihaspati, another name for Jupiter, teacher of the gods. Jupiter's exaltation is strongest in this nakshatra, which is considered one of the most auspicious. I think the fact that Saturn rules a nakshatra in Cancer, while Moon rules one in Capricorn, indicates a subtle connection between these two most different planets. Moon is personal while Saturn is impersonal and detached, yet if these planets are downcast they can both become attached. Saturn is the planet of concentration and Moon also is focused, but often on feelings and on our ego. Moon is watery and intuitive, while Saturn is earthy, methodical, disciplined, and oriented to wisdom, especially in Aquarius. I think Saturn in Pushya contributes to Cancer some of its power of focus. Saturn can be traditionalist and skeptical, so it can become dogmatic. If its energy is directed downward, then this nakshatra can perhaps be a bit dogmatic – in fact Cancer can be opinionated.

However, Pushya's true nature is nurturing, a renown characteristic of Cancer, the sign of mother. One of the symbols of this nakshatra is the lotus, beauty which rises from and above water. The lotus is a common symbol in India, denoting purity of mind rising from the waters of attachment and desire.

The last nakshatra of Cancer, *Ashlesha*, is also fully contained in it, as nine lunar signs map to four solar signs. The ruler is Mercury and the deity the Nagas, beings which have human and snake traits and symbolize wisdom as well as the poison of attachment to duality. Ashlesha is that part of Cancer which can be excessively and negatively attached. In this sense it reminds of Mercury's placement in Cancer, which loses clarity of mind because of reactive emotions and desires.

A symbol for Ashlesha is a coiling snake, alluding to the constrictive species of snakes. Somewhat similarly, Cancer's symbol is a crab, which has pincers. However, if the tenacity and grasping instinct of Ashlesha and Cancer are directed in a spiritual way, Ashlesha gives a profound and perceptive mind – Cancer is a water sign and can be very intuitive.

It is said that Buddha had his ascendant in Ashlesha. I've also read that Rabindranath Tagore had exalted Jupiter in Ashlesha, with Moon and ascendant in Pisces. I expected the mystical poet to have a strong Pisces, while Ashlesha shows the grasping strength of his intuitive perceptions.

The next nine nakshatras begin with *Magha* in Leo. Magha is ruled by Ketu and its deities are the Pitris, the divine ancestors and protectors of humanity. Yogananda had ascendant and Moon in Magha, and even though he was a spiritual master, in his autobiography he never identifies himself as such. He always expresses his devotion to the greatness of his guru and other spiritual masters, which we can identify with the Pitris. Kriyananda also has Moon in Magha and in turn he refers all his work as coming from Yogananda and God, without taking any personal merit.

At the same time, Magha is royal and magnetic: both Swamis speak with authority and confidence. A symbol for this nakshatra is a royal throne. Magha is the part of Leo which is confident, magnetic and assertive. Ketu is the planet which keeps a record of the past, and in this sense it supports Magha by referring its authority to a spiritual lineage of preceding masters.

An ideal king is wisely involved with every aspect of its kingdom, while a lesser king can be proud, controlling and demanding recognition; in either case, Magha indicates world involvement. If we always remember that our accomplishments do not come from our ego but from guru and God, then we won't become proud if we receive recognition, and we will be able to transcend the ego

Chapter Thirty

and find freedom from the material world. Lahiri Mahasaya, who belongs to the same lineage of spiritual masters of Yogananda, had the ascendant ruler, Venus, in Magha.

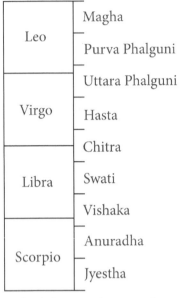

Second group of nakshatras. The second nine nakshatras correspond exactly to the middle four solar signs.

Purva Phalguni is also fully in Leo and it is ruled by Venus, the creative and joyful planet. The deity is Bhaga, a cheerful solar deity of prosperity which distributes good karma, each to their own merit. Leo is the 5th sign, and the 5th house is a benefic trine house, where we receive good karma from the past. Purva Phalguni is the part of Leo which is creative and radiating with self-expansion to inspire greatness in others. The symbol is a resting place, like a seat by the fireplace: Leo is fixed and comfortable in itself. Venus and Sun can be passionate, but as long as we don't become lazy and attached to the things we enjoy, Purva Phalguni reminds us of the simple and true happiness of just being in our true Self.

The next nakshatra, *Uttara Phalguni*, has one pada in Leo and three in Virgo; it is ruled by Sun and its deity is Aryaman. Aryaman is a generous solar deity with a focus on wisdom and dharma, the righteousness of our actions. As the aspect of Sun which cycles day and night, he has the duty to keep the flow of time, a responsibility which requires precision. In the Bhagavad Gita, Krishna says he is Aryaman, supreme light in the astral world and principal of the Pitris, the deities of Magha.

The inspiring light of wisdom and discrimination is potentially possessed by both Leo and Virgo. Leo shares it through being a radiating example and through counseling, meanings of the 5th house. Virgo applies it to questioning its own mind – or that of others. Uttara Phalguni is ruled by Sun, so in this nakshatra, in either sign, we should remember to not impose our will on others, even with good intentions.

Hasta is entirely in Virgo and it is ruled by the Moon; its deity is the solar Savitar. Savitar is the life-giving aspect of the Sun and is invoked in the powerful Gayatri mantra, a mantra that can be used in the fire ceremony for purification. A story narrates how Savitar's daughter, Savitri, was so pure and wise that she was able to convince Yama, the god of death, to bring her husband back to life. The symbol of Hasta is a hand, representing the ability to place in our hand what we are seeking. Virgo is the practical mutable earth sign of Mercury, it can be skilled and agile of mind and hand; it is also the sign of purity of mind – these are traits of Hasta.

The Moon is softer than the Sun, which makes Hasta more receptive than Uttara Phalguni. Hasta likes to grasp things. My wife's cousin is just one year old and she has Moon in Hasta. She loves to grab things and bring them to you; most kids like to do that but she seems to have a special fondness for it. She also likes to give them away as soon as she has them, because of her generous Jupiter in Pisces. Mercury's exaltation is strongest in Hasta, as it represents purity of perception.

Chitra is half in Virgo, half in Libra, and it is ruled by Mars. Its deity is Tvashtar or Vishvakarma, the universal builder, who counts among his creations the golden palace of Lanka, made for Shiva and his wife, as well as the thunderbolt weapon of Indra, king of the gods. Mars, the planet of energy and incisive perception, is similarly related to engineering. The symbol is a bright pearl, which is beautiful but takes time to build, layer after layer.

Chapter Thirty

The inspired effort and drive for perfection of Chitra is present in both Virgo and Libra: Virgo laudably strives to achieve perfection, sometimes to a fault; Libra's desire is for inner harmony and a chance to share it with others. Mars is dynamic and lends energy to this nakshatra.

After writing this paragraph, I noticed that Moon, Mars and exalted Saturn were in Chitra. Moon was in Virgo and I was concentrating hard, trying to understand as perfectly as I could the energy of this nakshatra.

Swati is fully in Libra, an air sign, and it is ruled by Rahu, an airy planet. Its deity is Vayu, god of the wind, but another deity closely associated with this nakshatra is Saraswati, the goddess of wisdom, knowledge, learning, art and science. A symbol for Swati is a grass leaf moving with the wind, signifying the harmony much loved by Libra. Libra is flexible but can also be too easily swayed. This nakshatra has a strong airy nature, so it can become restless, just like in Kriyananda's description of Libra. Libra, if rushing from one extreme to the other in an effort to find balance, can become the most unsettled sign of the zodiac.

Rahu is driven and it receives strength from Vayu, the deity of prana and father of Hanuman. Hanuman is the ideal example of pranayama; apart from his skill in battle and enormous strength, he was a talented writer and devotional singer, surely with the blessing of Saraswati. These associations show the idealism and creative knowledge of Swati and Libra. Yogananda had Ketu in Swati in the 3rd house, and Venus in Scorpio: he was a mystical poet.

Vishaka has three padas in Libra and one in Scorpio; it is ruled by Jupiter and it has two deities: Indra, king of the gods, and his twin brother Agni, god of fire. Indra wields lightning and is the father of Arjuna, fiery self-control in the 3rd chakra. Lightning is the purest form of fire. In *Avatar: The Last Airbender*, only few of the fire nation are able to control and channel lightning, as it requires peace of mind and calmness, unlike normal fire.

Indra, like Arjuna, balances the worldly duties of a king with the spiritual dharma of a divine being. Lahiri Mahasaya, the yogi householder, had ascendant and Jupiter in Vishaka, in Libra, and observed a similar balance between family duties and those of a renunciant.

Agni and his wife Swaha are considered that aspect of God which burns impurities offered into the fire of wisdom, either during the physical fire ceremony, yajna, or in the metaphysical yajna of Kriya yoga. Kriya meditation is a form of pranayama, the yoga discipline of the air chakra, the chakra of Libra and Taurus. Agni is connected to pranayama and the fire ceremony, in fact it also rules Krittika, a nakshatra which is 3/4 in Taurus. Agni and Swaha accept our devotion and bring it to God. The last word of most mantras is either swaha or namaha; swaha signifies offering our devotion into the purifying fire of wisdom, while namaha means to bow with receptivity and humility.

Indra and Agni are fiery and have great power, but fire is not the most sensitive element. In one story Indra is vexing Vishvakarma to keep improving a palace that the divine architect has built for him; the other gods stop Indra's inappropriate behaviour, teaching him a lesson in humility. I think it's interesting that Vishvakarma is the deity of Chitra, which bridges Virgo and Libra, and the drive to perfection (a characteristic of that nakshatra) leads Indra to insensitivity. This is a trait Kriyananda ascribes to Libra: in putting its inner harmony first, it can become unaware of the difficulties of others. Virgo can rather be too aware of the difficulties of others, in a judgemental way.

Vishaka links Libra and Scorpio, and Scorpio as well can be a bit insensitive, all the way to ruthless, in fact, as it is a sign of Mars while Libra is ruled by sensitive Venus. The exaltation of Saturn, the planet of detachment, is strongest in Vishaka: its deities symbolize self-control and selfless offering, while Jupiter's energy balances Saturn, making it stronger. Similarly, Jupiter's exaltation in Cancer is strongest in the nakshatra ruled by Saturn. Saturn in the sign of Venus also becomes softer and kinder.

In any case, Vishaka is ruled by benefic and expansive Jupiter, so its strength is primarily directed in a selfless way: Agni is said to selflessly carry the offerings of the fire ceremony to God, while Indra is a protector of the gods. Indra's chief accomplishment was to destroy a powerful demon who had stolen all the waters

Chapter Thirty

of the world. Because of freeing the waters, Indra is considered also a god of rain and thunderstorms. His fire is not as apparent as the fire of Agni, it is inner fire. Agni also rules Krittika, but that nakshatra is ruled by Sun and is more fiery: Jupiter softens Vishaka by comparison.

Vishaka is that purity of purpose common to Libra's dedication to harmony and Scorpio's focused intensity in its every effort. Kriyananda's Saturn is in Vishaka, in Scorpio, and his capacity for focus is awesome. Adelle's Moon is also in Vishaka in Scorpio, and she can be quite single-minded.

Anuradha is contained in Scorpio and is ruled by Saturn, the planet of concentration and focus. Its deity is Mitra, a solar deity of commitments and friendships. This nakshatra is focused on relationships and can be intensely devotional. Radha, the beloved companion of Krishna, is sometimes associated with this nakshatra and sometimes with Vishaka. This is probably because she had purity of purpose as well as intense devotion, in her relationship with Krishna. Radha symbolizes intense love for God. Depth of commitment, whether to spirituality or materialism, is a fundamental trait of Scorpio.

A symbol for Anuradha is the lotus, the flower of purity. Radha's commitment to Krishna is pure, without any possessive attachment, but this nakshatra is ruled by Saturn, the planet of attachment as well as detachment – so Anuradha can become attached, depending on our state of mind.

Jyestha completes the second group of nine nakshatras, ending together with Scorpio. It is ruled by Mercury and its deity is Indra, king and protector of the gods. Jyestha means eldest, excellent, or principal. In the Bhagavad Gita, Krishna identifies himself, among the gods, as Vasava (Indra), all-conquering and above dualities.

When the nakshatras are personified as 27 sisters, Rohini in Taurus is considered the most charming, while Jyestha, opposite in Scorpio, is the eldest. The firstborn brother and sister in India are revered and considered as a secondary father and mother; Yogananda mentions in his autobiography how unusual it was for his eldest brother to accept him as a guru. Two symbols of this nakshatra, the umbrella and the earring, are objects which indicate status and protection in old India.

The eldest sibling receives authority as well as a higher status, but has the responsibility to protect the younger siblings; from this sense of responsibility may originate some attachment and unwillingness to let go. Jyestha is the part of Scorpio which is self-possessed, but it also has the potential to become negatively attached. Similarly, Scorpio is rather protective of its own creative ideas and hidden subtlety of thought. Mercury gives subtlety, and as a symbol the eldest sister is ideally more thoughtful, perceptive, and dependable than her younger siblings.

Indra is the father of Arjuna, who symbolizes self-control and self-discipline, perhaps most needed in Scorpio among the twelve signs. In fact, Indra also rules Vishaka, making it the deity of more than half of Scorpio; this the highest side of Jyestha: self-mastery.

Adelle has Saturn in Jyestha, and Saturn rules her 9th house of spirituality as well as the 10th of public action. Adelle expresses the spiritual side of Saturn as 9th ruler, striving to achieve self-mastery, and also the practical side as 10th ruler, wanting to be a doctor. She's thinking of specializing in women's health and pregnancies, which in a way would make her a protective elder sister. If, instead of traditional medicine, she becomes interested in spiritual healing, she could also fulfill a similarly helpful role.

Yogananda had Venus, the benefic teacher of those who still have desires, in Jyestha; it is the ruler of his 3rd house of personal motivation, communication and writing, and of the 10th house. Yogananda is like a divine eldest sibling, protecting those who follow his teachings and encouraging us to become self-possessed.

The last nine nakshatras start with *Mula* at the beginning of Sagittarius. Mula means root or origin. The center of our galaxy, the Milky Way, lies in the direction of the stars of this nakshatra. The core of our galaxy is full of stars, certainly with an impressive night sky; Sri Yukteswar said it has a higher spiritual vibration than that of our solar system, which is located about two thirds of the way out. He explained that the Earth goes through cycles

Chapter Thirty

of higher and lower ages, called Yugas, depending on the location of the Sun, which moves periodically closer to the center of the galaxy before edging away again. Having only recently come out of Kali Yuga, the most materialistic age, we are currently in Dwapara Yuga, the age of energy, moving towards the galaxy center and a progressively higher consciousness for the whole planet.

Mula is ruled by Ketu and its deity is Nirriti, the goddess of dissolution, much akin to Kali, wife of Shiva. This is the part of Sagittarius which can be a little blunt in its enthusiasm, and a little destructive, wishing to impose its values onto others. However, the true purpose of Nirriti, much like that of Rudra in Ardra, is to dissolve negativity; this is a necessary step in the search for universal awareness of Sagittarius, but one that needs receptivity

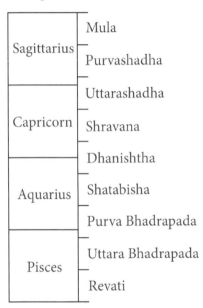

Third group of nakshatras. The third nine nakshatras correspond exactly to the last four solar signs.

to avoid becoming too destructive. Receptivity does not often come naturally to fire signs. That is why this nakshatra can be harsh in its intensity until we learn, like a positive Ketu, to forgo our ego and be receptive to higher insight.

Purvashadha is also fully in Sagittarius. It is ruled by Venus and its deity is Apah, the cosmic waters, though it is also often associated with Varuna, god of the ocean, or even with his wife Varuni, goddess of the purifying nectar of immortality. Water is a cleansing and revitalizing agent; sometimes yogis will meditate in a river, floating in surrender to divine will. Water is a receptive element, helping to make Sagittarius, a fire sign, very receptive to higher and universal truths, the search of which is its primary motivation. To merge with the waters of cosmic consciousness is to become pure, dissolving limitations and blocks, a process that is liberating and joyful. Venus, the nakshatra's ruler, is the planet of joy.

Ashadha means invincible and untiring. This is the part of Sagittarius which is enthusiastic, tireless and cheerful. The Sun of Yogananda, his ascendant ruler, was in Purvashadha: he was enthusiastic and joyful. If we want to find this joy ourselves we should practice his teaching: "Happiness comes, not by aimlessly thinking about it, but by *living* it in all the moods and actions of life."

Uttarashadha has one pada in Sagittarius and three in Capricorn; it is ruled by Sun and the deities are the Vishvadevas. This word is sometimes used to indicate all the gods together, but in this case it refers to the ten sons of Dharma. In some stories, Dharma figuratively opposes Kali, as she signifies dissolution of negativity and destruction of ignorance, while Dharma is usually more constructive. But that is a superficial distinction, because Dharma is also Yama, god of death. In his aspect as Dharma, however, his ten sons symbolize universal concepts which sustain dharma, such as truth and steadfastness. Yogananda, commenting on the verses of the Bhagavad Gita which describe the vision of God experienced by Arjuna, describes the Vishvadevas as aspiring hermits and as godly beings honored for their austerities in the Himalayas. The Himalayas symbolically represent the heights of spiritual consciousness.

Ashadha means invincible and tireless, but where Purvashadha is ruled by Venus, Uttarashadha is ruled by the Sun. Venus is the planet of the pranayama chakra, so it can indicate life-energy,

Chapter Thirty

but it is softer than the Sun. The Sun is fiery and has a projecting nature, giving great energy to this nakshatra. Uttarashadha is that part of Capricorn, the active earth sign, which has untiring determination. Sagittarius also has this trait in its own way.

Shravana is fully in Capricorn and it is ruled by the Moon; its deity is Vishnu. Vishnu maintains the structure of the universe, in fact Capricorn is the active earth sign and likes to act with a structured and organized approach. A symbol for Shravana is three footprints, from the story of Vamana, an avatar of Vishnu. In the story, the demon Bali had overtaken the whole universe, but he also had an honorable side, to which Vishnu appealed in the form of the young priest Vamana, requesting as much land as he could cover in three steps. Bali granted his wish, but was then dismayed to see the boy enlarge to such size as to cover the universe in just two steps; humbled, he bowed, offering his own head for Vishnu to lay his foot on, to complete the third and last step. Serious dedication to duty, like that of Bali willing to lose the universe to keep his word, is characteristic of this nakshatra and of Capricorn.

Krishna, another avatar of Vishnu, has a strong Rohini, which is a nakshatra also ruled by the charming Moon; appropriately, Vamana defeats Bali not through strength but wit and charm.

Charm is a form of magnetism, the power to attract and bring anything into realization; to realize things is certainly a drive of Capricorn. Kriyananda mentions how Capricorn can have an often unsuspected, charming sense of humour, the other side of its realism; I think this is also due to the Moon's softening influence on this nakshatra.

Capricorn, as the earth sign of Saturn, has a keen sense of reality and great skill for concentration; Moon also can be very focused in its own way. Shravana means ear, another symbol of this nakshatra; the ear concentrates sounds and also represents listening, an act of concentration. Shravana is the concentration necessary to accomplish our tasks, and in a deeper sense for listening to God's whispers.

The next nakshatra, *Dhanishtha*, is half in Capricorn, half in Aquarius; it is ruled by Mars and its deities are the eight Vasus.

Nakshatras

Their names change depending on the account, but they are basically elemental in nature: fire, earth, wind, sky, space (ether), light (Sun), water (Moon) and the stars. In the Bhagavad Gita, Krishna says that among the Vasus he is Pavaka, purifying fire; Yogananda comments that the Vasus are eight vitalizing deities or intelligent forces, among whom Pavaka, also called Agni, god of fire, is supreme.

The Vasus are a group deity, as opposed to Agni being the singular deity of Krittika, for example; this stresses their impersonal reality as universal elements. The only other group deity is the Vishvadevas, whose nakshatra, Uttarashadha, is between Sagittarius and Capricorn. The last four signs of the zodiac, starting from Sagittarius, are the most universal in nature.

In one story the Vasus briefly incarnate as offsprings to Ganga, the deity personification of the holy river Ganges; seven of them dissolve back in the river, but the eighth remains as Bhishma, one of the warriors of the Bhagavad Gita. Yogananda explains that Ganga represents the spiritual consciousness of God in creation, differentiated in eight parts. One part is the universal Spirit shining everywhere in creation. Six parts are conscious forces which rule different aspects of the universe, divided into the causal (ideas), astral (energy), and physical worlds; their names are Ishvara, Hiranyagarbha, Virata, Prajna, Taijas and Vishva. The eighth part is the reflection of Spirit in creation, or ahamkara, ego, personified as Bhishma. Normally, ego is related to the Moon, a personal principle, but Bhishma symbolizes the universal ego, so it is detached.

Dhanishtha is detached, a trait common to Capricorn and Aquarius, signs of Saturn. Even Mars, the ruler of this nakshatra and not known for its detachment, is here under the influence of impersonal forces which discipline and channel its strength into dharmic actions: Mars' exaltation in Capricorn is strongest in Dhanishtha.

Dhana means wealth, and Dhanishtha is often translated as very wealthy, however sanskrit is a subtle language. I am easily reminded of Sri Yukteswar's dry comments on the misunderstood translation of nasikagram in the Bhagavad Gita (root of the nose),

Chapter Thirty

which many take as advising the yogi to meditate cross-eyed, gazing at the tip of the nose, while it actually refers to the spiritual center between the eyebrows. Capricorn can certainly be very successful in accomplishing its goals; Satya Sai Baba had debilitated Jupiter in Dhanishtha, and he received millions of dollars in donations. However, a general interpretation of Dhanishtha as material wealth does not seem appropriate, because Jupiter is debilitated in this sign. The planets that are strongest in Capricorn, Mars and Saturn, are not renown for their material generosity; it is a definite possibility, but they are not like Venus and Jupiter. It is more accurate to refer to Dhanishtha as that wealth of good karma, whether material or spiritual, which is brought by following dharma. Similarly, Aquarius can be a fruitful sign in its own way, as it is the 11th in the zodiac, and the 11th house is the house of gains.

My Mars, which in my chart forms a Raja yoga and participates in a Kalpadruma yoga, is in Dhanishtha in Aquarius, perhaps enhancing the possibility of those yogas coming to fruition.

In any case, success and accomplishments can bring egoic attachment, which is the negative side of Saturn and of this nakshatra.

Shatabisha is entirely in Aquarius; it is ruled by Rahu and its deity is Varuna, god of the ocean, the vast waters of cosmic consciousness. The symbol for Aquarius is a water bearer, symbolizing its humanitarian desire to share knowledge with others. Shatabisha means a hundred healers, and is that part of Aquarius which seeks knowledge and uses it for service and healing. The highest expression of Rahu is selfless service.

The lowest expression of Rahu, however, can be forceful and compulsive. The same could be said for Mars, the ruler of Dhanishtha. Both nakshatras are in a sign of Saturn, a planet which, if negative, can become dogmatic – the planet of focus can become too focused and constrictive in its ideas. As a consequence in Aquarius, or with Saturn in general, we can try to impose our beliefs onto others, like a dogmatic priest or doctor convinced of the superiority of their knowledge. But with the detachment and honesty of true wisdom, Aquarius can be very positive. Sri Yukteswar had his Moon in Shatabisha.

Purva Bhadrapada is three padas in Aquarius and one in Pisces; it is ruled by Jupiter and its deity is Ajaekapada. Here we have another example of uncertain sanskrit translations. Bhadra means auspicious and pada means a few different things, one of them being foot, but it is also a generalized term for a portion of something, like a quarter of a nakshatra; it also means step like in Drupada. Eka means one, so ekapada can mean one foot, in fact a couple of hatha yoga positions which involve either standing on one foot, or grabbing one foot, have ekapada as part of their name. Ajaekapada is said to be an aspect of Shiva: in India there are statues of Shiva with a single leg, reminiscent of the tree pose in yoga, which requires good balance and interiorization to stand on one leg without swaying. Standing on a single leg also streamlines the human body into a straight line, symbolically significant if we remember the importance of a straight spine in yoga, opposed to duality and materialism.

The other root of Ajaekapada's name, aja, means unborn, uncreated, as a- is used to negate and ja means born, like in Panchajanya, the conch of Krishna. Aja is an adjective sometimes referred to deities and divine avatars like Krishna, because they are perfect expressions of God, who has never been born or created. But aja is also translated as goat, so several astrologers commonly accept that Ajaekapada means one-footed goat. Not surprisingly, they consider it a rather mysterious figure. Many deities have a vehicle, for example Durga rides a lion, and one of the few descriptions of Ajaekapada given by these astrologers is that it is a vehicle for the fire god Agni.

Now it may be true, but I doubt that this interpretation is correct; after all, virtually every Vedic expert believes we are still in Kali yuga, even after Sri Yukteswar explained how that belief originated, and clarified that we are actually in Dwapara yuga. Ideas, once established, are hard to change, and no publicly available evidence really exists to support the notion that Ajaekapada is a one-footed goat.

Ajaekapada has also been described as an ancient fire dragon, paired with the deity of the next nakshatra, Ahir Budhnya, a water dragon and an aspect of Shiva as well. In the ancient texts

Chapter Thirty

they are often named together, and dragon-snakes in a way only have one foot.

Drupada thinks that the goat represents the determination of this nakshatra, and that standing on one foot signifies centering on the unmanifest; traditionally Purva Bhadrapada is considered as having a fiery determination in upraising our energy.

None of the ideas above is really conclusive, though.

I think the meaning of Ajaekapada may be found in the sanskrit roots of its name, representing the universal nature of Spirit. In Shravana we have seen that Vishnu, the sustainer of the worlds, covers the whole universe in two steps, maybe symbolizing the duality of creation. Shiva represents the dissolution of creation back into the one Spirit, so perhaps that is the meaning of ekapada, covering the universe in one step, signifying unity and omnipresence.

A hint in that direction is found in the Indian tradition of vastu, which describes energy patterns in buildings. Vastu divides a building into a grid of equal squares, for example into 9 x 9 = 81 squares; the specific division with only one square for the whole space is called ekapada.

Yogananda explained that nothing exists outside of the one Spirit, so to create the universe God is using Maya, a cosmic illusion which separates the one Spirit into innumerable parts. Maya means the measurer because it measures, or divides, the universe into small parts. The generalized meaning of ekapada is one measure, standing in contrast with the many measures of Maya. Ekapada then suggests unity and universality, and in this context the best translation for aja is uncreated.

All deities are simply different aspects of God, and I believe Ajaekapada is meant to represent the Infinite, without origin and without separation. Shiva means auspicious, just like bhadra, and represents universality and transcendence, so it is fitting for Ajaekapada to be an aspect of Shiva.

Purva Bhadrapada, ruled by expansive Jupiter, is that blessed and auspicious pull towards infinity and expansion of our consciousness, common to both Aquarius and Pisces, the most universal signs of the zodiac.

Uttara Bhadrapada is fully in Pisces; it is ruled by Saturn and its deity is Ahir Budhnya, Shiva in the form of a water dragon which lives at the bottom of the deepest ocean. Considering the lack of extensive knowledge surrounding Ajaekapada and Ahir Budhnya, this deity may not actually be a dragon, but the idea seems to fit with the symbolism of this nakshatra, representing the depth of feeling that is a fundamental characteristic of Pisces, the mutable water sign of Jupiter, of compassion and universal empathy. Pisces has an inclination to not put itself in the spotlight, similarly to the 12th house, and Ahir Budhnya lives hidden in the depths of consciousness.

As an oceanic being, the water dragon is comfortably surrendered to the waters, reminding of the sensitivity and openness to feelings of Pisces. In its highest expression, this sensitivity is intuitive in a non-intellectual way, and blooms into natural devotion for God, which eventually becomes unshakeable thanks to the focusing influence of Saturn. The inspired poet Rabindranath Tagore had Jupiter in Ashlesha and the ascendant in Uttara Bhadrapada.

The last nakshatra is *Revati*, ruled by Mercury; its deity is Pushan, a nurturing solar deity. This nakshatra is friendly, compassionate, nourishing, and caring, all traits of Pisces. Mercury is a sociable planet, especially in the watery sign of Jupiter. Pisces is not so good for intellectual concentration, that is why Mercury is debilitated here; however it can make Mercury more intuitive.

Revati is the strongest part of Pisces for exalted Venus. Kriyananda has Venus in this nakshatra. Rabindranath Tagore had his Moon here. Yogananda's Jupiter was here as well, in his 8th house. Adelle's Jupiter and Rahu are also in Revati, following her guru's inspiration for friendliness and compassion. Revati means to move beyond, an apt meaning for Pisces and the 12th house of liberation.

Chapter Thirty One

Nakshatras and vimshottari dasha

There is another way nakshatras are connected to the vimshottari dasha system, apart from determining the ruler of the first dasha. Drupada explained that, very simply, the dasha sequence starts from the nakshatra of the natal Moon, and each subsequent dasha is linked to the following nakshatra.

For example, I was born with Moon in Ardra, in my 11th house, Gemini. The first dasha is then ruled by Rahu, the ruler of Ardra. As the next dasha, Jupiter's, begins, the next nakshatra activates; this is Punarvasu, ruled by Jupiter, which is 3/4 in Gemini and 1/4 in Cancer, my 12th house. Saturn's dasha is then linked to Pushya, while Mercury's will be to Ashlesha, still in my 12th house.

This connection can help interpreting the dashas. My Jupiter's dasha was mostly in the 11th house, a kama house of desires, and my natal Jupiter is debilitated, so it wasn't a very productive time. The following dasha, Saturn's, is completely in the 12th house, which hasn't always been easy. I had to move across the globe several times, changing country being one of the meanings of the 12th house. However it has also been very good for spiritual growth, and I've had many beautiful things happen in my life: Pushya, the nakshatra of Saturn in my 12th house, is most auspicious and nourishing.

As another example, Adelle's first dasha was Jupiter's in Vishaka, but Saturn's dasha started shortly after. This dasha had some traits of Anuradha, the nakshatra following Vishaka. Anuradha has intensity of feeling and friendship, something which has been relevant for her for most of that dasha. Recently she changed to Mercury and left her family home for the first time: Jyestha, ruled by Mercury, symbolizes self-possession.

Chapter Thirty Two

Chart calculations

Preparing a chart used to involve several mathematical calculations, but nowadays it's easily done with a computer. All that is necessary is the time and place of birth. The birth time needs to be as accurate as possible. If it is off by a few minutes it usually does not matter much, but if it is wrong by half an hour it could easily change the ascendant, changing all houses and most of the chart interpretation. If we are not sure of the ascendant we have to find it in an experiential way, by feeling its energy intuitively. To start with, we can try to feel which of the four elements the ascendant is, reducing the choice to three signs. The ascendant often determines our most immediate and spontaneous reactions, but if another sign is very strong it could confuse our perceptions. In that case, the best thing is to look at the houses and try to fit them to what we know of the person. Asking for inspiration during meditation is also greatly effective.

For example, Anne's ascendant (on page 39) is right between Virgo and Libra, changing with a time difference of only a couple of minutes. Virgo and Libra are quite different: one is very precise and questioning, the other diplomatic, perhaps a little airily aloof at times, but always subtly searching for harmony. After reflecting on the description of both signs made by Kriyananda, it was quite clear to me and her daughter that Anne's ascendant was Libra.

To calculate a chart, at the time of writing I use a free software called Jagannatha Hora; you can easily google and download it. I might write my own software in the future. Drupada has been using Shri Jyoti Star, which costs a few hundred dollars. Jagannatha Hora is very close to Shri Jyoti Star in giving the position of the planets and the dashas, however you need to be careful when determining the exact time zone of birth as it can be incorrect

Chapter Thirty Two

(nevertheless I am grateful to the author). I usually go to www. timeanddate.com and research the time zone and daylight saving for the year and country I am interested in. I think Shri Jyoti Star is accurate by itself in that regard. If you are interested in other astrological calculations which I do not use, like shadbala, then the two software give different results; it might be worth then to buy Shri Jyoti Star as it is probably the most accurate.

In Jagannatha Hora, simply run the software, press the Data button, and enter the time and place of birth. You can even enter the geographic coordinates directly, as they might be inaccurate for some countries. The chart will be done instantly, but there's another important thing to check first: the ayanamsha (under Preferences).

The ayanamsha is a measure of the difference between the tropical zodiac of Western astrology and the sidereal zodiac of Vedic astrology. Many arguments exist about the correct value of the ayanamsha; I use that of Drupada which is derived from the teachings of Sri Yukteswar. For the year 1973 it is 22 degrees and 18 minutes. It changes by about 1 degree every 72 years, or 0.83 minutes per year. I just add or subtract 0.83 minutes per year, so for the year 2013 that would be 0.83 times 40 years, or about 33 minutes. In 2013 the ayanamsha will then be 22 degrees and 51 minutes.

The ayanamsha most commonly used in India is that of Lahiri (not the master Lahiri Mahasaya) and sometimes the difference is significant. For example, in my chart Venus is at the threshold between Aries and Taurus; with Lahiri's ayanamsha it goes into Aries, but with Drupada's it goes into Taurus.

The chart of Kriyananda is a good confirmation of Drupada's choice. Both Moon and Saturn are right on the edge between two signs. With Lahiri's ayanamsha, Saturn is in Libra and Moon in Cancer; with Drupada's they are in Scorpio and Leo. I think it is obvious to anyone who knows Kriyananda that he has a royal personality, just like Moon in Leo. Choosing between Cancer and Leo changes the Moon nakshatra, and in Leo the Moon is in Magha. Magha is the same nakshatra of the Moon of Yogananda and it denotes a royal personality. Both Swamis are charming and

Chart calculations

radiating light, like a true Leo. Cancer can also be charming but its expression is different, softer and nurturing, with kinder and less willful magnetism. Cancer also enjoys familiarity, while Leo stands slightly apart, like a king. Kriyananda is compassionate but he is generally more detached than familiar. I am making a subtle distinction, because both Cancer and Leo are personal in expression, when contrasted with Saturn's signs which are impersonal.

Obviously, Kriyananda's detachment comes from his spiritual practice. Those with Moon in Cancer can also be detached but Cancer is a water sign of feelings; think of Kriyananda's mind, is it water or fire? I think it radiates light like fire. Water would be nurturing like Divine Mother. Look at any picture of Anandamayi Ma, she has that soft loving quality, in fact she was born with exalted Jupiter in Cancer. It's possible she also had Venus in Pisces and Moon in Scorpio, other water signs, depending on her birth time. In any case, the water element is evident in her appearance. At the same time, especially when answering metaphysical questions, she could be extremely impersonal, always referring to herself as "this body" – she had exalted Saturn. But you can always feel the soft, nurturing, watery energy of Anandamayi Ma.

Kriyananda has beautiful water qualities as well, having exalted Venus. Venus and Pisces can be artistic and this side of his chart becomes more evident when he speaks about his music. Otherwise, his speech feels invested with the implicit authority characteristic of Leo. Changing the Moon position from Cancer to Leo also moves it from the 2nd to the 3rd house, and the 3rd house is a strong communication house, especially of writing; he has written over a hundred books. If Saturn were in Libra it would be the 9th ruler exalted in the 5th house. Drupada observes how it is such a good placement for a yogi that he would have much fortune in his spiritual works. Saturn would be exalted in a trine house from the ascendant, and in an angular house from the Moon – a strong Saturn yoga. Kriyananda has been successful in spreading the teachings of Yogananda, but he had to work hard for it, and surmount many obstacles. That is best explained by having the 9th ruler in the 6th house, the house of efforts.

Chapter Thirty Three

Interpreting a chart

I have done my best to write much of what I learnt about astrology. There could be more to talk about, but it would not exhaust the many different possible combinations of planets, signs and houses: we have to develop our intuition to be able to interpret them. A systematic categorization would not necessarily be that useful; the only reliable way is to learn the basics and interpret them anew each time.

In a way, interpreting a chart is akin to finding which of the innumerable good spiritual teachings is best suited for a specific person at the moment of their reading. All the teachings from the masters are excellent to practice, but probably some will be just the thing that we need to hear in that moment. A good astrologer should try to find that special thing to say.

Yogic astrology is not focused so much on prediction, because we want to change the future for the better, and if it's already good, then we want to make it spiritually excellent. A good astrological reading is meant to encourage and inspire us to quicken our pace towards God, by improving our self-knowledge and introspection. It is not always easy to read a chart without sounding like a critic, but a beginner astrologer has to take that risk, to practice. Speaking with kindness is essential.

Throughout this book I wrote that this planet or that sign does something or another, but it was always shorthand to avoid repeating every time that it is our response to the stars that determines what happens in our life, and the stars are but an agent of the consequences of our past actions. In the renown comic strip, *Calvin and Hobbes*, Calvin asks Hobbes, his stuffed tiger, if he believes that our destinies are determined by the stars; Hobbes replies no but Calvin says he does. Hobbes seems surprised and

Interpreting a chart

asks why, to which Calvin replies: "Life's a lot more fun when you're not responsible for your actions."

No matter how tempting to think so, the planets are not responsible for our adversities, not even Saturn. Ultimately, we are not responsible either, it was God who seemingly separated our consciousness from His, and wants us to remember the Truth, that our union with Him has never changed.

We need compassion and kindness to interpret a chart, and a sense of humour. I keep in mind what Drupada says about the need for astrologers to be positive: if they come to us for a reading and we tell them negative things, it would be best for them if they had never met us! The same is true if we read our chart and we become overly worried about a weak planet, as if it were a personal failing, while forgetting the benefic influence of others.

Another thing to keep in mind is to watch for our own biases. In our chart some signs or planets inevitably give us more challenges than others, but when interpreting another chart we should detach ourselves from our experiential preconceptions. Astrology is the science of detachment and the art of seeing the Truth about energetic habits.

Yogananda said:

"Most human beings refuse to be guided from within, by higher wisdom. Instead, they live influenced by the deeply entrenched habits they created in the past. Their lives, in consequence, are like balls struck at the player's whim. As the ball in a game must go where it is sent, so mankind, habit-driven, has no choice but to live out the results of his karma as dictated by his own former actions.

Most human beings are slaves to their conditioning, which may appear as an outward cause but in fact has its origin within themselves. They are controlled by their habits. Although those habits were created initially by themselves, a habit, once formed, is self-perpetuating.

Very few people have any idea how insidiously their action-generated habits of the past influence their present behavior, their mental outlook, the companions and environment they attract, and what they mistakenly call their 'luck,' whether good

Chapter Thirty Three

or bad. They cannot see those habits welling up from deep in the subconscious mind, nor how they silently affect all their present attitudes and actions. People – Westerners, especially – believe they have free will. Others – mostly Easterners – imagine just as erroneously that there is no way out, that all is Kismet: Fate.

But there is a way out! That way is to renounce the false notion that we demonstrate freedom by giving free reign to our egoic desires. In Karma's realm, Karma rules supreme. Yet human beings have the power to withdraw to another realm altogether, by attuning themselves with the infinite wisdom behind karmic law. This much freedom is ours eternally: to accept God and His guidance from within, or to continue to be guided by our egoic desires.

The more we live guided from within, the greater our control over outer events in the great game of life. For when we live at our own center, in superconsciousness, we live in the only true freedom there is. In soul-consciousness we are no longer helplessly controlled by habits and desires. To the extent, then, that we develop soul-consciousness, we free ourselves from karmic slavery.

Instead of accepting fatalistically the decrees of karma, follow the inner way to freedom. Meditate daily. Commune deeply with God. Learn from Him, through the silent voice of intuition, the way out of soul-degrading serfdom to habits.

How long – how tragically long! – have habits kept you fearful about the future. If unexpected fortune and misfortune in your life confuse you, seek the only solution there is to life's endless puzzle: deep meditation, and increasing attunement with wisdom through daily contact with the ever-free, Infinite Spirit."

References

Your Sun Sign as a Spiritual Guide, by Swami Kriyananda. Crystal Clarity.

Autobiography of a yogi, by Paramhansa Yogananda. Chapter 16 is on astrology. A free version is available on the website of Crystal Clarity, which publishes the original, first edition.

The Wisdom of Yogananda series is published by Crystal Clarity and comprises several wonderful volumes, including: 1. *How to be happy all the time*, 2. *Karma and reincarnation*, 3. *Spiritual relationships*, 4. *How to be a success*, and 5. *How to have courage, calmness and confidence*.

Awaken to superconsciousness, by Swami Kriyananda. An amazingly clear book on several yoga concepts, such as yama and niyama. Crystal Clarity.

The Art and Science of Raja Yoga, by Swami Kriyananda, explains the connection between chakras and yoga. Crystal Clarity.

God talks to Arjuna: the Bhagavad Gita, by Paramhansa Yogananda, published by Self-Realization Fellowship. An inspiring book, even though it has been excessively edited by SRF, making its style a bit heavy. A lot of information on the metaphorical meaning of the personages who appear in the Gita. SRF also has several recorded talks of Yogananda.

Paramhansa Yogananda, a Biography, by Swami Kriyananda. Crystal Clarity.

Chakras for starters, by Savitri Simpson. Crystal Clarity.

Whispers from Eternity, by Paramhansa Yogananda. Crystal Clarity.

The Holy Science, by Swami Sri Yukteswar. SRF. Contains an explanation of the Yugas.

Avatar: The Last Airbender. The episode with the explanation of the elements is in Book 2, Earth, Chapter 9.

Hanuman, by Vanamali, published in USA by Inner Traditions. She also wrote *Shakti*.

The Second Coming of Christ, by Paramhansa Yogananda. SRF. It's been unduly edited, even more so than the commentaries on the Gita, making it quite heavy to read. However, it still has some inspiring passages.

Asha's articles can be found on the Ananda Palo Alto website, while those of Jyotish and Devi are on the Ananda village website. You'll also find many recorded talks there.

There are several recordings of astrology classes by Drupada; a short class should be freely available on Ananda Palo Alto's website.

You may contact the author at:

astrologyforayogi@gmail.com

Jai Guru

Printed in Great Britain
by Amazon.co.uk, Ltd.,
Marston Gate.